The Myth
of Family Decline

The Myth
of Family Decline

*Understanding Families
in a World
of Rapid Social Change*

Edward L. Kain

Lexington Books
D.C. Heath and Company/Lexington, Massachusetts/Toronto

Library of Congress Cataloging-in-Publication Data

Kain, Edward L.
  The myth of family decline : understanding families in a world of
rapid social change / Edward L. Kain.
     p.   cm.
  ISBN 0-669-13703-0 (alk. paper). — ISBN 0-669-13825-8 (pbk. :
alk. paper)
  1. Family—United States—History.   I. Title.
HQ535.K35   1990
306.85′0973—dc20   89-13427
                                                                                        CIP

Published simultaneously in Canada
Printed in the United States of America
Casebound International Standard Book Number: 0-669-13703-0
Paperbound International Standard Book Number: 0-669-13825-8
Library of Congress Catalog Card Number: 89-13427

The paper used in this publication meets the minimum requirements of
American National Standard for Information Sciences—Permanence of
Paper for Printed Library Materials, ANSI Z39.48-1984. ∞™

Year and number of this printing:

90 91 92 10 9 8 7 6 5 4 3

The childhood of Mildred Nelson Kain and Victor Oscar Kain was shaped in the crucible of the Great Depression. Their young adulthood was molded by the second World War. Like many American couples, they had several children during the post-war baby boom. I was the youngest of those children. My perspective on life was shaped by theirs. This book is dedicated, with love and appreciation, to my parents.

Contents

Tables

Acknowledgments

The conception, growth, and development of a book is seldom the product of one person's work. In the years leading to this final manuscript, a number of people have been crucial in shaping its form. Although it is impossible to thank all of the people who have influenced my thought and added to this book, I would like to thank those who were most important.

My interests in sociology and family change were first sparked by Verne Bechill, David Lemmen, and Irene Linder in the Department of Sociology at Alma College when I was an undergraduate. It was deepened and broadened by the faculty at the University of North Carolina at Chapel Hill, whose dedication to teaching and research showed me the strength of our discipline. In particular, John Reed, Ron Rindfuss, Peter Uhlenberg, Everett K. Wilson, and Robert Wilson all influenced my sociological imagination, and that effect can be seen interwoven in these pages.

My most important intellectual debts go to three people whose work inspired me when I read it as an undergraduate, nurtured me as I was a graduate student, and continues to affect my perspective when I now count them as colleagues. Gerhard Lenski, Jr. served as much more than my dissertation chair. His theoretical formulations provide the foundation for my approach, and his support throughout my career has been more than any student could hope for. He continues to stand as a model of a researcher and teacher who cares deeply for his students and his discipline. Glen H. Elder, Jr. helped me to appreciate the importance of a cohort approach, which links individual lives to the broader historical and social structure in which they are enmeshed and through which they move. His guidance when I worked at the Boy's Town Center, and later, when he was my colleague at Cornell University, has challenged me to link the macro- and micro-perspectives in new ways. The third person to whom I owe particular thanks is Sandra Bem, whom I was lucky enough to have as a colleague and friend in my years at Cornell University. Long before we met, her work made me think about gender in a new way, and her perspective continues to inform my research.

Many people have supported me along the way by reading manuscripts, challenging my ideas, and asking insightful questions. Among them are colleagues and students from Cornell University and Southwestern University: Steve Ceci, Andrea Parrot, Steve Cornelius, Elaine Walker, Tom Luster, Diane Wolf, Niall Bolger, Geraldine Downey, Jay Coburn, Diana Divecha, Ritch Savin-Williams, Urie Bronfenbrenner, Andrea Hunter, Mark Bongiorno, Joan Doughty, Shelly Immel, Shannon Hart, Sharon Birch, and Paula Eastman. Of particular importance has been the support of Gwen Kennedy Neville and Dan Hilliard, my colleagues in the Department of Sociology at Southwestern University.

Support for some of the work in this manuscript has come from the New York State College of Human Ecology at Cornell University and the Cullen Faculty Development Program at Southwestern University in Georgetown, Texas.

Finally, I would like to thank my editor at Lexington Books, Margaret Zusky, who helped me over the past several years as the book moved toward completion.

These people and many others have added to the strengths of this book. The responsibility for any weaknesses must remain my own. I thank them all, along with the many other colleagues, students, and friends who are a part of these pages.

Part I
What Is the Best
Way to Think
About Family Change?

1
Prophets of Doom

Almost daily, the headlines scream out yet another message that seems to indicate the family is on its deathbed in modern America. News magazines include stories on unprecedented rates of divorce, frightening reports of elderly Americans (seemingly forgotten by their family and society) being mistreated and neglected in nursing homes, and children being raised in single-parent families. The evening news talks about the majority of mothers working outside the home and of social movements supporting concerns as diverse as abortion rights and homosexual freedom. All these issues seem to signal that the basic institution in our society is threatened.

These challenges to the family have been met sometimes with dismay and sometimes with resignation, but in recent years they have also been met with counterattacks led by groups rallying around a battle cry for a return to the traditional family of the past. It appears that the war has begun. Those fighting in the trenches, however, are not at all certain of the outcome because there are many separate battles being waged at once.

This book is an attempt to step back from the apparent battleground of the closing decades of the twentieth century and evaluate the health of the family in the United States from a broader perspective—one that places current family life within the context of social change. Families do not exist in a vacuum, and we cannot begin to understand the quality of family life in the last decade of the twentieth century unless it is placed within historical and social context. What were American families like in the past? How have families been changing over the past century? What types of family patterns can we expect to see over the next several decades?

Unfortunately, the task of placing family life within a broader context is an assignment with many dangers. Because most of us were born into families and have spent most of our lives in the context of our own family structures, we all have some sense that we are knowledgable on the topic of family life. It is somewhat difficult to step back from our personal experience and evaluate the institution of the family with objectivity.

To understand families in the present or the future, we must understand families in the past. We cannot possibly assess the health of family life as we near the twenty-first century unless we place it within a broader span of historical time. As individuals and as a culture, however, Americans tend not to think of contemporary issues in historical perspective. This is true not only of popular accounts of family life, but also of the work done by many family scholars as well (a point to be discussed more in chapter 2). Like Rip Van Winkle who awoke to a world vastly different than that to which he was accustomed, we often look upon contemporary family life with dismay. Our world is changing rapidly, and many of these changes seem to challenge our very conception of family life. We long for a return to traditional values and the traditional family structure that we remember from the past.

This dismay at the current state of affairs and desire to return to the past is what I have come to label the "myth of family decline." Our image of families in the past is often based on myth rather than reality. For the past three decades, work by historians, demographers, and sociologists has begun to paint a new picture of the history of family life. Using innovative methods to explore church, family, and civil records, these researchers have discovered patterns of family experience that stand in stark contrast to the images many of us have held about the traditional family.[1]

As an illustration of this point, take the following quiz, which asks a few basic questions about family life both in the past and the present.

A Brief Quiz on Families and Change in the United States

1. Which of the following years had the highest divorce rate in the United States?
   A) 1935
   B) 1945
   C) 1955
   D) 1965

2. T   F   Because of the rapid rise in the divorce rate, children are much more likely to live in a single-parent household than they were a century ago.

3. T   F   In the past, most families lived in three-generation households. It is now much less likely for this to occur, since grandparents are put into nursing homes instead of cared for in the home.

4. What proportion of women worked outside the home in 1900?
   A) one in fifty
   B) one in twenty
   C) one in ten
   D) one in five

5. T   F   Over the past one hundred years, fewer and fewer people have been getting married, so the number of single people has been increasing.

6. T   F   The high incidence of female-headed households among black families today can be traced to the impact of slavery on family life as well as to the disruption of two-parent, nuclear families among black Americans during the time of Emancipation.

7. What is the most common household type in the United States today?
    A) a single-parent family with one adult wage earner
    B) a two-parent family with one adult male wage earner
    C) a two-parent family with two adult wage earners

8. T   F   Very few families live below the poverty line (as officially defined by the federal government) for extended periods of time (five consecutive years).

Before I give the results to this quiz, there are two things to keep in mind: First, don't be upset if you did not score very well. I have given this quiz to hundreds of students and professionals, and the typical result is that scores are extremely low. In fact, when I gave the quiz at a conference attended only by professionals who specialize in working with and teaching about family life, most of the questions were answered incorrectly by a majority of the group! Rather than being a statement about the quality of professionals in the area of family, this reflects the tendency of our culture to ignore the past and to base opinions about our basic social institutions (family, education, economy, religion, and government) on a cultural image that often is greatly at variance with reality.

Second, I want to suggest that each of these questions illustrates a basic point that will be discussed in this book. Now, for the answers to the quiz:

Question 1. Which of the following years had the highest divorce rate in the United States?: A) 1935; B) 1945; C) 1955; D) 1965. The correct answer to this question is B. No, that is not a typographical error in the book; the correct answer is 1945. Most people are very surprised that the correct answer is not 1965. "Isn't it true that divorce rates have been rising throughout the century?", they ask. This response clearly illustrates one of the first central points of this book: *We seldom have a historical understanding of family life or of the impact of specific historical events on the functioning of families.* The divorce rates in this country reached a historical peak at the end of World War II. Several explanations have been given for this: First, it is likely that a number of couples married hurriedly after relatively short courtships when the man was about to be sent off to war. Second, the stress of separation may have resulted in the development of other relationships for both the women at home and the men who were away. Third, both spouses may have changed considerably during the war years. The man who returned home from the battlefields may not have been the boy who left, and the woman at home may not have been the same girl whom he had courted and married. While it is true that divorce rates in this country consistently increased from 1950 through 1980, they did not match the peak of 1945 until the mid-1970s.[2] (See chapter 4 for further discussion about divorce and how it has been changing in this country.)

Question 2. (True or False) Because of the rapid rise in the divorce rate, children are much more likely to live in a single-parent household than they were a century ago. This statement is false. Most people do not realize the profound effects on family life that have resulted from rapid declines in the mortality rate since the turn of the century. While divorce has increased throughout this century, the drastic decline in the number of parents who die at an early age (leaving widows, widowers, and orphans behind) more than offsets the increase in single-parent households that results from marital disruption caused by divorce.[3] This question reflects a second basic principle of the book: *If an adequate understanding of family change is to be developed, we must look not only at data from the past but also at the relationships between different types of changes affecting family life.* (See chapter 4 for an elaboration of this idea.)

Question 3. (True or False) In the past, most families lived in three-generation households. It is now much less likely for this to occur, since grandparents are put into nursing homes instead of cared for in the home. This statement is false for a number of reasons. One of the most important findings of the new family history has been a challenge to the idea that the rise of the modern nuclear family (the family including only two parents and their children) is linked to industrialization and is a result of that process. Peter Laslett[4] and others have demonstrated that, at least in England, the nuclear family was the dominant form of household long before the advent of industrialization. Laslett makes a strong argument for the continuity of family life over time, and suggests that in a number of ways the family in the "world we have lost" was much as it is today. This illustrates a third central point of the book: *When we have actual data about family life in the past, it often presents a picture of family life that is drastically different from the image that is common in popular mythology.*

In fairness, I must say that Laslett's work is a reaction to most contemporary theories of the family, which ignore the importance of historical time. Unfortunately, Laslett's approach has been criticized for ignoring the dynamic nature of the family as a group. Just as the institution of the family has changed over historical time, individual families change over the family cycle. Subsequent work has suggested that while at any point in time most families in preindustrial Europe may have been nuclear in structure, if families are traced over their developmental cycle, many of them are extended for brief periods while the elder parents are still alive.[5]

Even if everyone wanted to spend part of their family cycle in a three-generation household, however, it still would not be possible for many families. First, only *one* of the children and his or her family typically lived with the elderly parents, so in every family there would be a number of siblings who would live in nuclear households. In addition, the elder generation seldom survived long enough to spend much time in a three-generation household (see chapter 3.)

Question 4. What proportion of women worked outside the home in 1900?: A) one in fifty; B) one in twenty; C) one in ten; D) one in five. If you chose answer D, you are right. Yes, fully one in five women worked outside the home in paid occupations at the turn of the century.[6] Many were employed as domestic servants and in agriculture. Others worked in textile mills and in teaching positions. Still others were employed in the new clerical sector, which was expanding as our country moved further into the industrial age. This growth of the female labor force is discussed more fully in chapter 5.

Most people are surprised that the female labor force participation rate was that high. We tend to have an image that women only started working outside the home during World War II, and that they returned home when the war ended. The rise of female labor force participation is often seen as a recent event linked to the women's movement of the 1960s. Certainly there has been an increase in the number of women working outside the home since 1950. In reality, however, the rate of female labor force participation has been rising relatively consistently since the late nineteenth century. This points to a fourth principle that will be repeated throughout this book: *Most of the changes occurring in families in the United States are not revolutionary but evolutionary—they are changes that have been happening gradually over a long period of time, and they do not represent a radical change from patterns in the past.*

Question 5. (True or False) Over the past one hundred years, fewer and fewer people have been getting married, so the number of single people has been increasing. The correct answer to this question is false. (By now you are probably catching on to the idea that your first guess may have been wrong.) Both the popular press and sociological research in recent years has focused on the increase in singlehood.[7] This increase, however, has only been happening since 1950, a period when more people married than any other time in all of American history. In essence, there was no place for the rate of singlehood to go but up. If a longer historical view is taken, it becomes clear that the rates of singlehood today are still lower than they were a century ago. (More on this in chapter 4.) This reflects a fifth basic point of the book: *When we do include history in our conceptions of family life, we tend to focus only on recent history and remain blind to the broader picture of social change and continuity in family life.*

Question 6. (True or False) The high incidence of female-headed households among black families today can be traced to the impact of slavery on family life as well as to the disruption of two-parent, nuclear families among black Americans during the time of Emancipation. This statement is false. While the reasons for the high incidence of single-parent, female-headed households among black Americans today may be complex, they cannot be traced to a legacy developed from the period of slavery and Emancipation. In a series of careful studies, Herbert G. Gutman[8] shows that between 1855 and 1880 as many as 90 percent of black households contained both a husband and wife or just a father with children. The matriarchal household was common neither among antebellum free blacks, nor among black families after Emancipation. The continuing myths about the causes and implications of the structure of black families illustrate another central point of this book: *Historical causes may be built into current explanations of family life, but unless data are used to examine the validity of these historical explanations, our understanding of the relationship between historical events and family life may be seriously flawed.* I might add to this statement the general observation that when groups that are not white, male, or middle-class are concerned, our historical understanding is usually less sophisticated and more often incorrect. The new family history has involved more attention to issues of race, class, and gender—much to the benefit of our understanding of family life in the past.

Question 7. What is the most common household type in the United States today?: A) a single-parent family with one adult wage earner; B) a two-parent family with one adult male wage earner; C) a two-parent family with two adult wage earners. This question turns from the history of family life to the contemporary family in the United States. Like the questions on the history of the family, it illustrates that we may have misconceptions about families in contemporary America. The correct answer is C. By far the most common type of household in the United States today is one in which both adults work outside the home.[9] (An elaboration of this can be found in chapter 5.) This illustrates that *no matter what family life was like in the past, in the contemporary United States the so-called traditional family is in a distinct minority.*

Question 8. (True or False) Very few families live below the poverty line (as officially defined by the federal government) for extended periods of time (five consecutive years). The statement in question 8 is true. Research using data from the Panel Study of Income Dynamics at the University of Michigan illustrates clearly that a very small percentage of families remain consistently below the poverty line (approximately 4 percent).[10] Rather, families move in and out of poverty as wage earners lose a job, are rehired, a divorce occurs, or additional children are born, changing the stresses upon the family budget. This clearly points to the fact that *our conceptions of the family as a static institution are inadequate, and we must think of families as dynamic groups that change over the lifetimes of the individuals who are involved.*

There is another quiz like this later in the book that concentrates entirely upon attitudes about sexuality and reproduction. For now, however, you can relax once again. No more tests for several chapters!

Many of these new findings in family history and family sociology have taken quite some time to find their way into textbooks in the social sciences—and even longer to reach the popular consciousness. Most of us still carry images of a mythic extended family of domestic bliss within our minds. It is important, however, to base our decisions about political issues related to families on reality rather than myth.

Partly because of the American tendency to romanticize the past, and partly because of the many changes in family life that seem so evident during the past several decades, it is common for social analysts to conclude that the family is, indeed, in trouble. Analyses that predict the demise of the family have come from both ends of the political spectrum. On the radical side, Christopher Lasch has suggested that the family is a failure as a "haven in the heartless world" of industrial capitalism, and he paints a gloomy picture about the future prospects of any improvement.[11] According to Lasch, the family is supposed to shield its members from the harsh realities of working life in modern society, and it has failed in this task.

Similarly, the New Evangelical Right fears that the traditional family is in serious danger. Groups like the Moral Majority preach against the sins of modern times and demand that we return to the core American values of the traditional family. The forces of the New Right have supported a variety of types of legislation that attempt to embody these so-called traditional values into the legal structure. Most notable among these attempts was the Family Protection Act, first introduced in September of 1979 by Senator Paul Laxalt. Later versions of the Family Protection Act were introduced to the House by Representative Hansen of Idaho and Representative Smith of Alabama in 1981, and Senator Jepsen of Iowa introduced a revised version to the Senate in June of the same year.[12] I have more fully discussed some of the provisions of the Family Protection Act elsewhere, and a full explication is not necessary here.[13] In essence, the goal of the legislation was to reinforce what is defined as the traditional family—based upon a mythical vision of peaceful family life under patriarchal rule, in which the husband is the breadwinnner and the wife is in the home raising the children.

While certainly the most comprehensive in scope, the Family Protection Act is not the only example of attempts in the 1980s to enshrine what is perceived as the traditional family in the laws of the land. Perhaps the most visible example has been the introduction of various versions of a Human Life Amendment, which would ban or limit legal abortion. All these measures can be seen as an attempt to shore up what is perceived as the crumbling foundation of the central institution of any society—the family.

Not everyone, however, agrees with the assessment that the modern family is in trouble. Some, such as Harvard sociologist Mary Jo Bane, argue that while families are changing, they are still vigorous and "here to stay."[14] Bane provides convincing evidence that ties between grandparents and grandchildren and between parents and children have, if anything, become stronger in recent times, rather than weaker.

One reason that the debate about the health of the family is such an important concern is the rapid rate of social change in our society. Changes in our culture create many social problems, as adjustments in some parts of the culture lag behind. William F. Ogburn's concept of cultural lag provides a useful tool for evaluating this problem.[15] As we have moved in the space of a century from an agricultural economy to a postindustrial society, our social institutions have had difficulty keeping up with the massive shifts generated by technological change. The resulting social problems are at the core of many of the political controversies seen today at the national level, including civil rights for people of color, women's rights, and homosexual rights.

Not surprisingly, many of these controversies center on the family: abortion and reproductive rights; homosexuality; the changing roles of women and men; day-care; and comparable worth (the idea that men and women should receive equal pay for jobs that are similar in content, not only for jobs that have the same job title). Because the family is a key institution in any society, and because the transition from agriculture to industry transforms the basic relationships between economic production and family life, many of the cultural lags demanding attention today are reflected in these national political issues.

Unfortunately, as is clear from this chapter, we are often blind to the realities of family life in the past. Our cultural images of family life in past times are difficult to change, even when data indicate the images are much more myth than reality. Like Rip Van Winkle, we long for a return to the good old days, when life was much simpler and times were happier.

We live with a myth of family decline—the notion that families in the past were stable and happy and that recent decades have seen a rapid decay of family life. The central goal of this book is to paint a more accurate portrait of how families in the United States have actually been changing, so we can better understand family life in the present and in the future.

This goal will be achieved by examining a series of questions that must be answered if we are to have a comprehensive understanding of family life in the twentieth century. The first question is, "What is the best way to think about families and social change?" After a basic framework for exploring family life has been established, we will turn to the question, "How have families in the United States *actually* been changing?" This exploration will be divided into several sections that correspond to some of the basic functions of the family as an institution: the economic function (women, men, and work, and the changing roles of both sexes); reproduction (abortion and reproductive rights, homosexuality); regulation of sexual behavior (attitudes toward sexuality, premarital and extramarital sex, homosexuality); and socialization and personality development (again, related to women and work, homosexuality, and abortion and reproductive rights).

Before we can begin to explore the past, present, and future of family life in the United States, we must answer the question, "What is the best way to think about change?" This is the question to which we turn in the next chapter.

Notes

1. See, for example, John Demos, *A Little Commonwealth: Family Life in Plymouth Colony* (New York: Oxford University Press, 1970); John Demos and Sarane Spence Boocock (eds.), *Turning Points: Historical and Sociological Essays on the Family* (Chicago: The University of Chicago Press, 1978); Michael Gordon (ed.), *The American Family in Social-Historical Perspective*, 3rd ed. (New York: St. Martin's Press, 1983); Philip Greven, *Four Generations: Population, Land, and Family in Colonial Andover, Massachusetts* (Ithaca: Cornell University Press, 1970); Herbert Gutman, *The Black Family in Slavery and Freedom,* (New York: Pantheon, 1976); Kenneth A. Lockridge, *A New England Town: The First Hun-*

dred Years, (New York: W. W. Norton & Company, 1970); and Theodore K. Rabb and Robert I. Rotberg (eds.), *The Family in History: Interdisciplinary Essays* (New York: Harper & Row, 1970).

2. For more complete data on trends in marriage, divorce, and remarriage, see Andrew Cherlin, *Marriage, Divorce, Remarriage* (Cambridge, MA: Harvard University Press, 1981).

3. See Peter Uhlenberg, "Death and the Family," *Journal of Family History* 5 (1980):313–320.

4. See Peter Laslett, *The World We Have Lost*, 2nd ed. (New York: Charles Scribner's Sons, 1971).

5. See Lutz Berkner, "The Stem Family and the Developmental Cycle of the Peasant Household: An 18th-Century Austrian Example," *American Historical Review* LXXVII (1972):398–418.

6. Historical data on female labor force participation in the United States can be found in a number of sources. See, for example, *The Statistical History of the United States from Colonial Times to the Present* (New York: Basic Books, 1976) and United States Bureau of the Census, *The Historical Statistics of the United States from Colonial Times to 1970, Bicentennial Edition* (Washington, DC: Government Printing Office, 1975).

7. See, for example, Peter Stein, *Single* (Englewood Cliffs, NJ: Prentice-Hall, 1976). The best example of media coverage on singlehood is the flurry of popular articles that quickly appeared after a 1986 study was released projecting the rate of marriage among college-educated women. Both *Newsweek* ("The Marriage Crunch: If You're a Single Woman, Here Are Your Chances of Getting Married," June 2, 1986) and *People* ("Are These Old Maids? A Harvard-Yale Study Says that Most Single Women Over 35 Can Forget About Marriage," March 31, 1986) carried extensive cover stories examining the plight of single women. Little mention is made of where these patterns fit in historical perspective.

8. See Herbert G. Gutman, *The Black Family in Slavery and Freedom* (New York: Pantheon, 1976).

9. See George Masnick and Mary Jo Bane, *The Nation's Families: 1960–1990* (Boston: Auburn Publishing, 1980).

10. Data from the important research resulting from the Michigan Panel of Income Dynamics can be found in a number of volumes, such as Greg J. Duncan and James N. Morgan (eds.), *Five Thousand American Families—Patterns of Economic Progress* (Ann Arbor, MI: Institute for Social Research, 1979).

11. See Christopher Lasch, *Haven in a Heartless World: The Family Besieged* (New York: Basic Books, 1977).

12. For different versions of this legislation, see The Family Protection Act bill H.R. 311. 1981; The Family Protection Act bill H.R. 3955. 1981; The Family Protection Act bill S. 1378. 1981; and The Family Protection Act bill S. 1808, 1979.

13. See Edward L. Kain, "The Federal Government Should Not Foster Legislation Relating to the Family," in Harold Feldman and Andrea Purrot, *Human Sexuality: Contemporary Controversies* (Beverly Hills: Sage, 1984).

14. See Mary Jo Bane, *Here to Stay: American Families in the Twentieth Century* (New York: Basic Books, 1976).

15. See William F. Ogburn, "Cultural Lag as Theory" in Otis Dudley Duncan, *William F. Ogburn on Culture and Social Change* (Chicago: University of Chicago Press, 1964).

2
The Importance of Perspective

How you analyze a problem depends largely on how you define the issue in the first place. Your way of looking at the world shapes the types of questions you ask, the data you collect to answer your questions, and the ways in which you analyze and evaluate these data.

Chapter 1 pointed out that many social analysts have concluded that the family in modern America is deeply troubled. As we saw, this conclusion may largely be a result of the many misconceptions about family life in the past. Many of these prophets of doom seem to be looking at families from a perspective devoid of historical and social context. How did such a perspective develop? More importantly, perhaps, what theoretical approach can avoid some of these misconceptions about family life in the past to provide a more accurate assessment of the basic health of American families?

As we begin to talk about perspectives for analyzing family life, it is important to think about the family in at least two ways: as an institution (the macro-level of analysis) and as a small group in which individuals spend much of their lives (the micro-level of analysis). Family sociology in recent decades has tended to concentrate on the family as a small group and has focused less attention on the family in relation to the rest of society.[1] This is one of the major reasons that the historical context of family life has remained unexplored for so many years.

It is misleading to focus on only one level or the other because families are essential both as an institutional structure that has functions in the larger society and as a group within which individuals are born, grow, and develop. For that reason, if we are to truly develop an understanding of families and social change, our theoretical approach must take both levels of analysis into account.

In this chapter I argue that the most useful way of thinking about family life is a model that combines insights and principles from neoevolutionary theory (as developed by Gerhard and Jean Lenski) at the societal level, with methods and concepts from life-course theory and cohort anal-ysis (as developed by Glen H. Elder, Norman B. Ryder, and a number of others) at the individual and group level.[2]

These two theoretical approaches are complementary for a number of reasons. First, both theories stress the importance of cross-cultural and historical evidence. Second, both theories concentrate on social change rather than social structure—or, more accurately, both stress that social structure is not static but dynamic. Third, both theories point to the importance of transitions. Neoevolutionary theory concentrates on transi-tions between levels of technological development within societies, and life-course theory points to the importance of understanding transitions in the life course of individuals. Fourth, both approaches point to the impor-tance of understanding stability over time as well as patterns of variation; both continuity and change are a part of human life.

The interested reader can learn more about each of these theories by consulting work by researchers in the area.[3] For the purposes of this book, I will briefly review some of the major principles of each theory. These will provide a foundation for the analyses that are found in the remaining chapters. Before turning to an examination of the usefulness of these two approaches, however, it will be instructive to briefly examine the ap-proaches that have dominated our understanding of family life throughout the past several decades.

Defining and Studying the Family

Several times in the introductory chapter I referred to the family as a central institution. By this I mean that the family serves a number of functions essential for the survival of any society. A critical debate within family sociology has been about how to define the family. Definitions vary considerably, depending on the theoretical tradition in which the re-searcher is trained. Those in the social conflict or Marxist tradition tend to see the family as an oppressive institution that reflects the power relationships and conflict inherent in the larger society.[4] Theorists inter-ested in the family as a small group are more likely to look at exchange relationships between members of the family or the subjective definitions of experiences in the domestic sphere.[5]

The dominant paradigm in sociology throughout much of this century has been the structural functionalist approach. While functionalism has been severely criticized for its tendency to support the status quo and its seeming inability to deal with processes of social change, the basic fact remains that at a macro-analytic level, functional analysis provides one of the most useful frameworks for understanding the structure and process of institutions within a social context.

Structural functionalism tends to define the family in terms of the basic functions that the family serves in society. The central functions usually identified include reproduction, regulation of sexual behavior, socialization of new members into society, economic and protective functions, emotional support and personality development, and placement of adult members in the social structure.[6]

The conventional wisdom has argued that the functions of the family have been shrinking over time. One of the first elaborations of this thesis was provided by William F. Ogburn.[7] Ogburn suggested that in preindustrial society the family served many more functions. In particular, he pointed to the decline of the economic functions of the family as industrialization moved work out of the home and into the factory. Lenski has illustrated how in hunting and gathering societies, the family is indeed the primary institution.[8] Many functions that we now associate with separate institutions, such as government, religion, education, and medicine, were within the family. As the technological level of societies increases, there is a gradual emergence of separate institutions, and the family becomes more specialized in its functions.

Some functionalists argued that the specialization of the family had developed to such an extent that the only functions remaining were socialization and the development of stable adult personalities.[9] Because these functions are at the social-psychological level, analysts like Talcott Parsons focused totally on the family as a small group and expanded the conception of specialization so that it was applied even to the roles within the family. He argued that industrial societies demand a mobile workforce, and the most efficient way to have a functioning family is to have men specialize in instrumental activities (goal oriented—such as earning a living) and women specialize in expressive activities (relationship oriented—such as raising children). Parsons's work is an excellent example of how functionalism can be applied in a way that seemingly justifies the status quo and what has come to be viewed as the traditional family.

There are several problems, however, with this basic analysis of what has happened to families with industrialization. First, Parsonian functionalism is largely ahistorical. There is little sense of the operation of dynamic forces that change society. Second, the focus on the family as a small group has meant that changes in family life are divorced from the broader social context within which families interact. Finally, the picture of a decline of functions of the family has all too often been interpreted as a decline of the family as an institution. As Clark E. Vincent has argued, however, the shrinking in functions of the family may also be interpreted as a positive movement that has increased the adaptability of families in a modern world that demands constant adjustment to the rapid rate of social change facing us daily. He suggests that it is incorrect to speak of a loss of functions; instead, the change has been in the form and content of the functions of the family. For example, while Ogburn and his associates concentrate on the loss of the economic function of the family, Vincent points out that the family is now a primary economic consumption unit, as opposed to its earlier role as a production unit.[10]

A number of theorists in this tradition have suggested that our images of family life in the past may not be accurate. Ogburn's concern is that analyses of family life should be based on data rather than speculation, and he notes that often we do not have the information necessary to accurately understand family life in previous centuries.[11] Perhaps the most important statement concerning the problems of relying upon a cultural image of blissful family life is found in William J. Goode's *World Revolution and Family Patterns*, in which Goode talks of the "classic family of Western nostalgia." Goode ends the functionalist analysis of family changes throughout the world with a call for truly archival research into the historical nature of family life.[12]

By the middle of this century, family sociology had seemingly reached a consensus. The family was viewed as rapidly changing under the impact of urbanization and industrialization. The institution was slowly losing its traditional funcitons until most of its remaining tasks were psychological. The key functions of the family were viewed as providing a stable environment for the development of children's personalities and socialization into adult roles. As a result, family studies focused on the micro-level of analysis and looked more deeply at roles and interaction within the family. Socialization and personality formation were important research topics, while history was largely ignored. This focus on contemporary society, as well as an almost complete concentration on the United States, was not limited to family sociology, but was found throughout the discipline.[13]

A major facet of this conventional wisdom (especially as formulated by Parsons and associates) was the functionality of the small, isolated nuclear family and a modern industrial society that demands mobility in the occupational structure.[14] William Goode's *World Revolution and Family Patterns* represents the most comprehensive attempt to evaluate the impact of urbanization and industrialization on the family. He not only attacks traditional idealizations of the family; he also asserts that sociology must address its problems from a cross-cultural perspective. Many of the sweeping generalizations of the conventional wisdom are seriously shaken when the investigator moves beyond the study of Western culture.

Nineteenth-Century Evolutionism and the Emergence of Functionalism

Another reason that functionalism tended to be ahistorical and to focus on the micro-level of analysis lies in the historical development of the functionalist paradigm. The structural functionalist model developed largely as a response to flaws in nineteenth-century evolutionary thought.[15]

Throughout the nineteenth century, theorists and researchers interested in family life shared a perspective that focused on long-term change in the structure of families. For these early evolutionists, both time and space were crucial dimensions. The family in different cultures and throughout the whole span of history was researched and debated. Indeed, debate and disagreement seemed to be a common characteristic of the classical evolutionists. This was to become one of the reasons for the rejection of evolutionary approaches to the study of the family. Many sequences of family development throughout the history of humankind were posited by these early theorists, and each of the theorists devoted a great deal of effort to defending his particular stance as well as to attacking his opponents. Despite the sometimes bitter debates, the evolutionists did share a number of characteristics.

The search for origins was a central concern of most of the classical evolutionists. It was asserted that the origin of an institution held the key to its subsequent development.[16] The evolutionists also shared the idea that society and its institutions would progress in moral as well as structural terms. For the socialists the ultimate progress depended on revolution; for others it was a result of natural selection.[17] Change was thus directional, and humanity was viewed as ultimately perfectible. Finally, these theorists also shared the contention that their evolutionary schemes were universal and necessary.

In his critique of the "comparative method," and of the Western theory of development in general, Robert Nisbet summarizes what the classical evolutionists shared. Change, Nisbet says, was viewed as natural, immanent, continuous, directional, necessary, related to differentiation, and a result of uniform processes. In addition, the work of the evolutionary theorists was largely concerned with questions of origin, stages of development, and questions of purpose or ultimate end.[18]

Around the turn of the century, the evolutionary theorists began to face severe criticism, and eventually evolutionary thinking was abandoned in favor of different approaches to studying the family. The rejection of evolutionary approaches to the study of the family resulted in largely static analyses of the family. History and the time dimension were for the most part ignored by researchers.

At the center of the attack on the evolutionary paradigm were theorists who developed the basic model of structural functionalism. Two major figures in anthropology, Franz Boas and Bronislaw Malinowski, played decisive roles in the development of the critique of classical evolutionism. The work of Boas pointed to the flaws in evolutionary thinking, and both men's work redirected research and formulated new questions that ignored some of the central concerns of evolutionism. In particular, the analysis of social change was transformed radically (if not practically eliminated) from the study of the family.[19] Both Boas and Malinowski stressed fieldwork and the importance of ethnological studies of existing societies. They are responsible for training many of the major figures in twentieth-century anthropology, including Margaret Mead, Ruth Benedict, Edwin Sapir, Melville Herskovits, Alfred Kroeber, Raymond Firth, H. L. Shapiro, M. Gluckman, Hortense Powdermaker, and Edward Evans-Pritchard.[20]

Within sociology there was a parallel move away from the study of history and toward a focus on fieldwork. The Chicago School of Sociology emphasized the idea of using the city of Chicago as a training ground and school. The move was away from broad theorizing and toward the empirical study of specific, concrete situations.

The history of the family was no longer a concern of the social theorists. For nearly half a century, the family of the past was not an object of research. When theories of social change and the family were considered, the conceptions of the family in the past were based on conjecture and idealization. Unwittingly, the functionalist school, which developed from the groundwork laid by Malinowski, as well as the interactionists in the Chicago School, suffered from the same flaw as the classical evolutionists. Conceptions of the family of the past were based on conjecture, and the foundation was laid for development of a myth of family decline within academia.

Neoevolutionary Theory and the Study of Long-term Social Change

As previously noted, by the middle of this century, a number of theorists and researchers began to question the image of family life in past time. Research evidence from a variety of sources also began to challenge the images of family life provided by the conventional wisdom. A small but dedicated group of French historical demographers, under the leadership of Louis Henry, began an examination of the demographic characteristics of pre-Malthusian populations throughout the decade of the 1950s. They devised a very powerful method known as *family reconstitution* to utilize the rich information found in French Catholic parish registers.[21] By the middle of the next decade, a group of British historical demographers, largely under the auspices of the Cambridge Group for the History of Population and Social Structure, applied and expanded these methods, using Anglican parish registers in the British Isles.[22] This early work of the historical demographers tended to ignore the life cycle of the family, but eventually the dynamic aspects of family at the micro-level were also built into the work that was being done.[23]

Evolutionary theories of social change also began to reappear in the 1960s. Despite claims of the critics of neoevolutionary theories, these theories differed radically from their earlier counterparts.[24] The various forms of neoevolutionary theory, while differentially stressing the roles of ideology and technology in the process of change, define evolution in terms of increased adaptation to the environment.

The evidence available to analysts of long-term social change has increased a great deal since the time of the classical evolutionists. While archaeology was in its infancy at that time, new methods of investigation in the field, including radiocarbon dating and satellite photography, have revolutionized the discipline.

The groundwork for materialist evolutionary theory (which points to the importance of technology in understanding social change) was formulated by writers such as V. Gordon Childe in Britain and Leslie White in the United States.[25] It was modified and refined by later writers, and has been most carefully formulated by Gerhard and Jean Lenski.[26]

Neoevolutionary theory, as outlined by the Lenskis, suggests that the transition between different levels of technological development is a major point at which changes occur in all the institutions of society. Thus, the transition from hunting and gathering to horticultural forms of economy had important implications for the structuring of family life. Similarly, the transition from simple horticultural systems to advanced agricultural systems with a large surplus also caused many changes throughout society as well as in the family. The most recent transition in technological level has been from agricultural to industrial. This transition (often labelled the Industrial Revolution) has had implications for family life that are just as profound as the previous transitions. The remainder of this book will examine the data concerning some of the changes in family life that have occurred as we have been moving from an agricultural to an industrial society in the United States.

The basic argument I will present concerning family life at the macro-level, or institutional level, is that changes in families can be linked to the transition from a traditional agrarian society to an industrial technological society. For the first time in human history, the advent of the factory system separated work from the home. With the Industrial Revolution in the West came the new conception of separate spheres of life—the world of work and the world of the family.

While a neoevolutionary model is the theory guiding the macro-analysis found in this book, the methods to be applied are historical and comparative. Since the focus of this book is on families in the United States, most of the analysis will be historical rather than comparative.

Life-Course Theory and Cohort Analysis

At the micro-level, the focus in this book will be on life-course theory and cohort analysis. Before this approach can be discussed, however, it is useful to examine how we more typically think about families at an individual level.

When we move to the micro-level, or small group level, most of us tend to think of social change and the family in terms of generations. When something is different for one generation than it was for previous generations, then we can measure social change.

There are, however, several problems with using generations to measure change. First, the concept of a generation does not refer to any specific length of time or number of years. Families vary a great deal. The Smith family may marry in their late teens and have their first child shortly after (or even before) marriage. If their children follow the same pattern, Mr. and Mrs. Smith may become grandparents before reaching the age of forty. Next door, the Jones's may get married in the same year as the Smiths, but when they are both in their late twenties. They may delay having their first child until their mid-thirties, and since their children do the same, they will be near the age of seventy when they first become grandparents. By this time, the Smiths next door will have great-grandchildren who are in junior high school. It is evident that comparisons of people within the same generation might be quite confusing.

Just as the years between generations vary between families, the years within a generation can be very wide. If a woman has her first child at the beginning of her reproductive years and her last child right before reaching menopause, there may be more than a quarter of century difference in the ages of the children within the same generation. The generations within one extended family may overlap considerably as a result.

Let me give you an example. I noted earlier that families in agricultural societies are very different than families in industrial societies. The same variation is found *within* a society. Rural families and urban families have traditionally been different on a variety of characteristics. One of these characteristics is fertility; farm families, in particular, have traditionally been larger than city families. Both my parents were born and raised on farms in rural Michigan. My mother had nine brothers and sisters and my father had seven brothers and sisters. All of the siblings who survived to adulthood married, and most of them had children. Some of them had a large number of children. Because of the span of years within both the parents' and the children's generations (my aunts and uncles and my cousins), some of my first cousins are almost as old as some of my aunts and uncles. If we move to the next generation, some of the grandchildren are older than some of my first cousins. Now it's getting confusing, right??

Thus, a second reason that the concept of generation is not very useful to the analyst of social change is that people in different generations (which are really units of kinship, not units of time within the family) may actually have more in common than people within the same generation.

Cohorts Rather than Generations. If the concept of a generation is misleading when we are studying social change, what is the alternative? At the micro-level, it is useful to think of cohorts rather than generations. A cohort is any group of people who experience something at the same time. Thus, you might talk of a work cohort, or everyone who starts to work at the same time. A marriage cohort would be all those who married in the same year. The most common use of the term cohort, however, is the birth cohort—everyone who was born in the same year. Because all those born in the same year share a variety of historical and social experiences, the birth cohort is an excellent marker for the study of social change. In his classic article on the utility of the concept of a cohort for studying social change, Ryder points out that differences between cohorts provide us with measures of social change, while differences within cohorts indicate social diversity.[27] The cohort concept is thus ideal for the study of family life, since we are interested both in diversity within a cohort and change between different cohorts.

This does not mean, however, that we should discard the idea of a generation. The kinship structure of families is clearly organized around generations, and patterns of interaction and support revolve around generations within a family. What I am suggesting is that we use the cohort as the marker of social change for comparing individuals within and between generations.

Your Family as an Example. As an example, use both the concept of a generation and the idea of a cohort comparison to look at your own experience. Ask yourself the following questions. How old are you? Are you currently employed? If so, what type of job do you have? What is your history of employment? How many years of education have you completed? How many brothers and sisters do you have? Did they all live until they reached adulthood? Are your parents still alive? Are they still married to each other? Were you born in this country? Is English your first language? Do you live on a farm or in a city?

Now, imagine that you are your same-sex parent. We are now moving back one generation. Ask the same set of questions. Was your same sex parent employed when he or she was your age? If so, in what type of job? What was that person's full employment history? How many years of education had he or she completed? How many brothers and sisters did he or she have? Did they all live until they reached adulthood? Were his or her parents still alive when he or she reached adulthood? Were they still married to each other? Was he or she born in this country? Did he or she live on a farm or in a city? By asking these questions, you can begin to see how the life experience of a member of your parent's cohort compares with your own.

Now move back yet another generation. Ask the same questions about your same-sex grandparent. Ask them about the grandparent of the other sex. The variation in these answers helps to illustrate within your family the rapid rate of social change as well as the variation within a cohort (by sex).

This exercise also points out that the simple measure of age is much more complex than it first appears. While age is certainly a measure of chronological age, it is also a measure of social and cultural time. Your chronological age places you in a particular position within the life course, with certain roles and obligations typically assigned to people of your age. These may change over historical time so that the expectations for a man or woman of age twenty-one in 1990 are very different than they were in 1890. Finally, age is also a measure of the cohort into which someone was born—a reflection of the unique historical and social experiences of a group of people moving through social and historical time.

The usefulness of the concept of a cohort, however, goes far beyond the experience of your family. Cohort analysis is an excellent tool for understanding the changes in our broader society. A few examples will illustrate how cohort analysis can help us to better understand the social world.

Applications of the Concept of a Cohort

The Baby-Boom Cohorts. One of the most striking illustrations of the impact of changes in the structure and composition of cohorts is the example of the baby boom. In the late 1940s and early 1950s, couples started having more babies than had been the case in the decades immediately preceding the second World War. Theorists and researchers have argued about the causes of this increase in fertility, but whatever the explanation, the simple fact is that the birth cohorts of the late 1940s and early 1950s were larger than the birth cohorts that had preceded them.[28] These babies were born into a world in which the postwar economic boom allowed many of their parents to build homes in the suburbs. Indeed, the larger birth cohorts demanded that more homes be built to accommodate the expanding population.

Companies that made diapers, toys, and baby food expanded as their clientele entered the market. Gerber Baby Foods became a multinational corporation in the 1950s. As the baby-boom cohorts aged, they affected every institution in American social life. The construction industry flourished, not only because new houses were needed, but also because new elementary schools were built to meet the demands of the expanding cohorts. More men and women went on to get college degrees, since teachers were needed to teach in the schools. Since the birth cohorts that preceded the baby boom were smaller, the job market was good, and the scarcity of teachers gave them bargaining power.

As we move to the late 1950s, the baby boomers were now the high school rockers. A new youth culture emerged in the United States, and construction continued to boom as more high schools were built. College and university faculty were needed to teach the teachers who were teaching the large cohorts of elementary and eventually high school students. The number of people going on for advanced degrees shot up sharply in the late 1950s and early 1960s to meet this growing demand.

It is important to place these large cohorts within historical time. When the baby boomers reached college age, because they were born during a relatively affluent period in American history, a larger proportion than ever before planned on going beyond high school to college. In 1950, only 14 percent of the population between the ages of eighteen and twenty-four was in college. Men in this age group were more than twice as likely to be in college than were women. (This would be the birth cohort of approximately 1929, born at the onset of the Depression). The children of these Depression cohorts, however, many of whom were in the baby-boom cohorts, faced a very different world. Over 32 percent of those between the ages of eighteen and twenty-four were in college by 1970, and the sex ratio was much closer to parity.[29]

In addition to entering college in larger numbers and from a background of affluence, these later cohorts entered college at a time when the United States was in an unpopular, undeclared war in Southeast Asia. Racial tension was strong throughout the country. Blacks sat in at the Woolworth's lunch counter, and dared to register for classes at the University of Alabama. Watts was torn by racial violence soon to be joined by other cities, and when the average American watched the evening news, it seemed that most of urban American was up in flames.

College antiwar protests spread across the country overnight, and many Northern white college students went South to march in the civil rights demonstrations. For the first time in the history of the country, a large proportion of the cohorts between the ages of eighteen and twenty-one were in college, and the force of their protest changed the shape of American politics throughout a decade of unrest.

In the Wake of the Baby-Boom Waves. As they moved through the life course, the large cohorts of babies born in the late 1940s and early 1950s clearly changed social institutions, and this continues to be the case. The cohorts that follow are much smaller. When the baby-boom cohorts begin to retire, there will be smaller groups of productive workers contributing to social security, and this has caused much concern in the popular press about the future solvency of this program. The effect on subsequent cohorts, however, began to occur much earlier than this.

As the baby boomers graduated from high school, smaller groups of students followed into the educational system. First there were partially empty elementary schools, and then empty high schools in cities and towns across the country. Many of these have been converted to shopping centers, co-op apartments, and community buildings, since the space was no longer needed for educational purposes. The college students who flocked to courses in education began to find themselves in a tight job market where there were too many teachers for too few jobs. Unlike the 1960s, when teacher shortages were common, bachelor degrees in teaching were a dime a dozen by the mid 1970s.

Just as fewer teachers were needed to teach the smaller cohorts, so too were fewer college professors needed to teach the teachers. The job market for Ph.D.'s became bleak so that by the end of the 1970s many highly educated people were underemployed.

Throughout the social structure, the shock waves of the baby boom were felt as this large group first entered and then exited from various stages in the life course. These highly trained baby boomers saturated the job market, so that the post-baby-boom cohorts of college-educated students faced much tougher competition when they picked up their diploma.

More recently, the baby-boom cohorts have reached the childbearing years. Although they have been more likely to delay having their first child, and their overall fertility rates are lower, because of the large size of the cohorts there is a ripple effect as their children again form larger birth cohorts. Teacher shortages are now beginning to occur, and within the next decade the demand for Ph.D.'s will increase as the children of the baby boomers enter college and graduate school.

Thus, we can see that something as simple as the size of a cohort can have major implications not only for the experiences of individuals within that cohort, but also for the cohorts that precede and follow it and for the very structure and process of institutions within society.

A Model for Thinking About Families and Social Change

A model that combined all the facets of neoevolutionary theory and life-course theory would necessarily use information from anthropology, history, sociology, and psychology. At the societal level, neoevolutionary theory as developed by the Lenskis covers the entire span of human history from the dawn of humankind through the present. At the individual level, life-course analysis as developed by Elder uses longitudinal data on individuals to trace the impacts of early life events on the later development of individuals.[30] The scope of each of these approaches is broader than the focus of this book. The data that are required at both levels simply are not available.

Thus, although insights from these two approaches will guide the analyses in this book, this is far from a complete synthesis of neoevolutionary theory and life-course theory.

The guiding principles that are drawn from these two approaches include:

1. A concern for historical and social context.

2. An awareness that most simple models distort social reality by oversimplifying the complexity of the interrelationships between variables in social life.

3. A concentration on points of transition: at the societal level, the transition from an agricultural to an industrial economy; at the individual level, transitions in the life course and in the family life cycle.

4. An analysis that thinks of social change as a process and conceptualizes structure as something that changes dynamically.

5. A concentration upon continuity as well as change, and an assumption that most changes are evolutionary and process-oriented rather than revolutionary and discontinous with the past.

Thus, the answer to the question, "What is the best way to think about family change?" is: At the macro-level, neoevolutionary theory and historical comparative analysis should guide the study of families and social change; at the micro-level, life-course theory and cohort analysis provide the necessary tools.

Now that we have developed a model for thinking about social change and families, we turn to the question, "How have families in the United States *actually* been changing?"

Notes

1. For a more detailed discussion of the history of family studies and the theoretical frameworks that have guided family research, see Harold T. Christensen (ed.), *Handbook of Marriage and the Family* (Chicago: Rand McNally, 1964) and Bert N. Adams, *The Family: A Sociological Interpretation*, 4th ed. (New York: Harcourt Brace Jovanovich, 1986). For coverage of developments in family

theory in recent decades, see Reuben Hill and Donald A. Hansen, "The Identification of Conceptual Frameworks Utilized in Family Study," *Marriage and Family Living* 22 (1960):299–311; Carlfred B. Broderick, "Beyond the Five Conceptual Frameworks: A Decade of Development in Family Theory," *Journal of Marriage and the Family* 33 (1971):152; and Wesley R. Burr, Reuben Hill, F. Ivan Nye, and Ira L. Reiss (eds.), *Contemporary Theories About the Family* (New York: The Free Press, 1979).

2. For a further explication of sociocultural evolution, see Gerhard Lenski and Jean Lenski, *Human Societies: An Introduction to Macrosociology* (New York: McGraw-Hill, 1987). An excellent application of life-cource theory and cohort analysis is found in Glen H. Elder, Jr., *Children of the Great Depression: Social Change in Life Experience* (Chicago: University of Chicago Press, 1974). Further explication of both theory and method in this tradition are found in John A. Clausen, *The Life Course: A Sociological Perspective* (Englewood Cliffs, NJ: Prentice-Hall, 1986); Glen H. Elder, Jr., "The Life-Course Perspective," in Michael Gordon (ed.), *The American Family in Social-Historical Perspective*, 3rd ed. (New York: St. Martin's Press, 1983), pp. 54–60; Phyllis Moen, Edward L. Kain, and Glen H. Elder, Jr., "Economic Conditions and Family Life: Contemporary and Historical Perspectives," in Richard Nelson and Felicity Skidmore (eds.), *American Families and the Economy: The High Costs of Living* (Washington, DC: National Academy Press, 1983), p. 213–254; Alice Rossi (ed.), *Gender and the Life Course* (New York: Aldine, 1985); and Norman B. Ryder, "The Cohort as a Concept in the Study of Social Change," *American Sociological Review* 30 (1965): 843–861.

3. See works cited in note 2, as well as Peter Uhlenberg, "Death and the Family," *Journal of Family History* 5 (1980): 313–320; and research cited in chapter 1, note 1.

4. For several examples of a Marxist perspective, see Christopher Lasch, *Haven in a Heartless World: The Family Besieged* (New York: Basic Books, 1977); Eli Zaretsky, *Capitalism, the Family, and Personal Life* (New York: Harper and Row, 1976); and Juliet Mitchell, *Woman's Estate* (New York: Vintage Books, 1973).

5. The classic statement defining the family as a small group is Ernest Burgess' "The Family as a Unity of Interacting Personalities," *Family* 7 (1926):3–9. Explications of exchange theory are found in Peter Blau, *Exchange and Power in Social Life* (New York: John Wiley & Sons, Inc., 1964) and F. Ivan Nye, "Is Choice and Exchange Theory the Key?" *Journal of Marriage and the Family* 40 (1978):219–233.

6. See Kingsley Davis, *Human Society* (New York: The MacMillan Co., 1963) for a clear outline of the functional perspective on the family institution.

7. Ogburn's perspective on the declining functions of the family can be found in William F. Ogburn, "The Family and Its Functions," in William F. Ogburn (ed.), *Recent Social Trends*, Chap. 13. (New York: McGraw-Hill, 1933) and William F. Ogburn and M. F. Nimkoff, *Technology and the Changing Family* (Boston: Houghton Mifflin, 1955). See also Ernest W. Burgess, "The Family and Sociological Research," *Social Forces* 26 (1947):1–6.

8. See Gerhard E. Lenski, *Power and Privilege* (New York: McGraw-Hill,

1966), pp. 100–101, as well as the Lenski and Lenski book cited in note 2.

9. See Talcott Parsons and Robert F. Bales, *Family, Socialization and Interaction Process* (Glencoe, IL: The Free Press, 1955).

10. This argument is developed in Clark E. Vincent, "Familia Spongia: The Adaptive Function," *Journal of Marriage and the Family* 28 (1966):29–36.

11. William F. Ogburn and M. F. Nimkoff, *Technology and the Changing Family* (Boston: Houghton Mifflin Company, 1955).

12. William J. Goode, *World Revolution and Family Patterns* (New York: The Free Press, 1963), pp. 366–367.

13. See Everett C. Hughes, "Ethnocentric Sociology," *Social Forces* 40 (1961):1–4.

14. See Talcott Parsons, "Age and Sex in the Social Structure of the United States," *American Sociological Review* 7 (1942):604–616, and "The Social Structure of the American Family," in Ruth Anshen (ed.), *The Family: Its Function and Destiny* (New York: Harper and Brothers Publishers, 1949), pp. 173–201.

15. For a further discussion of the development of functionalism as a response to nineteenth-century evolutionism, see Harold T. Christensen (ed.), *Handbook of Marriage and the Family* (Chicago: Rand McNally, 1964) and Edward L. Kain, "Early Evolutionary Perspectives and the Study of the Family" (Paper presented at the 1980 meetings of AKD, Richmond, Virginia, February, 1980).

16. See Johann Jakob Bachofen and Ralph Manheim (trans.), *Myth, Religion, and Mother Right: Selected Writings of J. J. Bachofen, 1861.* (Princeton, NJ: Princeton University Press, 1967).

17. For examples of a socialist perspective, see Robert Briffault, *The Mothers* (New York: Macmillan Company, 1927), and Frederick Engels, *The Origin of the Family, Private Property, and the State* (New York: Pathfinder Press, 1972, originally, 1884). Examples of those on the natural selection side of the argument are Herbert Spencer, *The Principles of Sociology*, Vol. I, Part II (New York: D. Appleton and Company, 1876), and Edward Westermarck, *The History of Human Marriage*, 5th ed. (New York: Allerton Book Company, 1922).

18. See Robert Nisbet, *Social Change and History* (New York: Oxford University Press, 1975).

19. For examples of the criticisms of evolutionism as well as the new approaches in anthropology, see Franz Boas, *Race, Language, and Culture* (New York: Macmillan, 1948) and Bronislaw Malinowski, *The Family Among the Australian Aborigines* (New York: Schocken Books, 1963, originally 1913). Discussions of the growth of early anthropology and the decline of evolutionism are found in Marvin Harris, *The Rise of Anthropological Theory* (New York: Thomas Y. Crowell Company, 1968), and H. R. Hays, *From Ape to Angel* (New York: Capricorn Books, 1964).

20. See the book by Hayes in note 19.

21. See Pierre Goubert, "Historical Demography and the Reinterpretation of Early Modern French History: A Research Review," *Journal of Interdisciplinary History* I, and "Local History," *Daedalus* 100:113–127; Louis Henry, "The Population of France in the Eighteenth Century," in D. V. Glass and D. Eversley (eds.), *Population in History* (Chicago: Aldine, 1965), pp. 434–456; and "Historical Demography," *Daedalus* 97:385–396.

22. See Glass and Eversley, cited in note 21. Also see Peter Laslett, *The World We Have Lost* (New York: Charles Scribner's Sons, 1971, originally, 1965), and Peter Laslett and Richard Wall (eds.), *Family and Household in Past Time* (Cambridge, UK: Cambridge University Press 1972).

23. A seminal article that points to the importance of the life cycle is Lutz Berkner's "The Stem Family and the Developmental Cycle of the Peasant Household: An 18th Century Austrian Example," *American Historical Review* LXXVII (1972):398–418.

24. Both Robert Nisbet, *Social Change and History* (New York: Oxford University Press, 1975, originally 1969) and J. D. Y. Peel, *Herbert Spencer, The Evolution of a Sociologist* (London: Heinemann, 1971) criticize the growth of neoevolutionary modes of thought. Gerhard Lenski in "History and Social Change," *American Journal of Sociology* 82 (1976):548–564, clearly outlines the differences between classical evolutionism of the nineteenth century and sociocultural evolutionism of the twentieth century.

25. See V. Gordon Childe, *Man Makes Himself* (New York: Mentor, 1951) and *Social Evolution* (London: Watts & Co., 1951); Leslie White, *The Science of Culture* (New York: Grove Press, 1949).

26. See Lenski and Lenski, cited in note 2.

27. See Norman B. Ryder, "The Cohort as a Concept in the Study of Social Change," *American Sociological Review* 30 (1965):843–861.

28. For one explanation of the baby boom, see Richard A. Easterlin, "The American Baby Boom in Historical Perspective," Occasional Paper 79. (National Bureau of Economic Research, New York, 1962); "On the Relation of Economic Factors to Recent and Projected Fertility Changes," *Demography* 3 (1966):131–153; and "Relative Economic Status and the American Fertility Swing," in E. B. Sheldon (ed.), *Family Economic Behavior* (Philadelphia: J. B. Lippincott, 1973, pp. 170–223).

29. *The Historical Statistics of the United States, Colonial Times to 1970*, Series H 700–715 (Washington, D.C.: U.S. Department of Commerce, Bureau of the Census, 1975), p. 383.

30. See Elder, cited in note 2.

Part II
How Have Families
in the United States
Actually Been Changing?

3
Farm Families and the Transition to an Urban-Industrial Society

The opening chapter of this book illustrated that Americans foster a number of myths about the family, including idealized images of family life in the past. The second chapter suggested some theories and methods that might be useful in looking at the data to assess our images of family life and to build a more complete understanding of families and social change. Most of the remainder of this book is devoted to applying this general model to answer the question, "How have families in the United States *actually* been changing?"

As noted in chapter 2, neoevolutionary theory suggests that change in American families is best understood when viewed in the context of the transformation of this country from an agricultural to an industrial economy. This chapter looks at this transformation and some of its implications for family life.

The Macro-Level

William J. Goode has suggested that the family acts as a mediator between the individual and the larger society.[1] The form, content, and process of *how* the family mediates between the individual and the larger society is directly linked to broad scale technological change. During the past several decades, family historians and historical demographers have begun to explore family life in "the world we have lost."[2] While these researchers are careful to point out the complexity of relationships among the variables involved in social change and family life, it is clear that a central facet of the transformation has been the movement of work from the household to other settings.[3] Central to this separation was the growth of the industrial system and the decline of agriculture as the main economic activity of American families.

Table 3–1 illustrates the continuous decline in the proportion of the U.S. population that was employed in agriculture from 1850 through

Table 3–1

Percentage Distribution of the Economically Active Labor Force by
Sector of Economic Activity: 1850–1980

	Agriculture	Industry	Services
1850	45.6%	23.8%	30.6%
1860	41.2	24.7	34.1
1870	46.5	21.6	31.9
1880	43.2	21.7	35.1
1890	37.5	24.3	38.2
1900	37.5	35.8	26.7
1910	30.9	38.2	30.9
1920	27.0	40.2	32.8
1930	21.2	39.6	39.2
1940	17.4	39.8	42.8
1950	11.8	41.4	47.1
1960	6.3	39.7	54.0
1970	3.1	36.3	60.6
1980	2.8	31.7	65.6

Sources: Data for 1850–1890 are calculated from *The Report on Population of the United States at the Eleventh Census: 1890*, Part II. (Washington, DC: Government Printing Office, 1897), civ–cviii. Data for 1900–1970 are calculated from *The Historical Statistics of the United States*, Series D 182–323. (Washington, DC: U.S. Department of Commerce, Bureau of the Census, 1985), 139. Data for 1980 are calculated from *The Statistical Abstract of the United States: 1984*. (Washington, DC: U.S. Department of Commerce, Bureau of the Census, 1983), 417, Table 693.

Note: The data vary: Data for 1850–1880 include workers who were sixteen or more years of age; data for 1890 include workers who were fifteen or more years of age; and data for 1900–1970 include workers who were fourteen or more years of age.

All of the tables in this book refer exclusively to the United States.

1980. Data from the mid-nineteenth century vary in their coverage. Only the free male population is included in 1850, only free males and females in 1860, and it is not until 1870 that the percentages are based on all workers in the U.S. population. The focus here is on broad issues of social change. The analysis is intended to provide the background and framework for more specific analyses of this transition from an agricultural to an industrial society, which is presented in later chapters. Thus, cross-sectional differences over time are examined, or inter-cohort comparisons are made. All the changes examined, however, vary by a number of factors, including race, class, gender, and region. Thus, the general principal that a shift from agricultural to industrial occupations affected families is true for all groups, but the exact nature of these effects varied by factors such as race and class. Some of these differences will be noted in later chapters, but the focus here is on inter-cohort variation rather than intra-cohort variation.

Accompanying the decline in the dominance of agriculture throughout this time period was the increasingly urbanized nature of the U.S. population. Table 3–2 illustrates that the proportion of the U.S. population that is rural (defined as living in areas with a population of less than 2,500) has steadily declined since the mid-nineteenth century. This long-term trend reversed itself for the first time in the 1970s, when there was a net migration to nonmetropolitan areas in the United States.[4] While the proportion of the population living in rural areas has steadily declined, the actual numbers of rural residents increased up through 1940. From that point on, there was a decline in actual numbers, with the trends again reversing in the 1970s.

It is important to point out that the linear trends in both these variables (percentage of the rural population in agriculture and percentage urban) are the result of a complex set of historical changes. They are not simply the result of the children of farmers moving into both non-agricultural jobs and urban areas, although this is an important part of the trends. The movement into the cities was not a simple process—often it took several generations. Many of the early migrants saw industrial jobs as a way of saving money to purchase farm land, and fully intended to return to the rural areas. Most studies of residential mobility in the mid-nineteenth century find that approximately half the urban population left the city within ten years.[5] In addition, successive waves of immigrants to the United States were differentially integrated into the occupational structure, and a disproportionate number of these immigrants entered American society as urban dwellers in non-agricultural jobs.

Both these trends have important implications for American families. As individuals and families move from rural to urban settings and from agricultural to non-agricultural occupations, at least two important sets of changes take place. First, the structuring of occupational roles and demands is altered. If we view the family as the mediator between the individual and the larger social system, it is occupational demands that represent a major link between work and family life. Shifts in one role are accompanied by alterations in other parts of the overall constellation of an individual's set of roles. Second, and this point is perhaps more intricately related to the first than we realize, a whole range of demographic and social variables are linked to both rural residence and being employed in agricultural occupations. Change in important family variables such as fertility is clearly linked with a move from rural to urban settings.[6] Rural families and households have higher marriage rates, a higher child-to-woman ratio, more children ever born and persons per household, and lower rates of divorce and female labor force participation than urban

Table 3–2
Urbanization: 1850–1980

Year	Rural		Urban	
	#*(in 1,000s)*	%	#*(in 1,000s)*	%
1850	19,648	84.7%	3,544	15.3%
1860	25,227	80.2	6,217	19.8
1870	28,656	74.3	9,902	25.7
1880	36,026	71.8	14,130	28.2
1890	40,841	64.9	22,106	35.1
1900	45,835	60.3	30,160	39.7
1910	49,973	54.3	41,999	45.7
1920	51,553	48.8	54,158	51.2
1930	53,820	43.8	68,955	56.2
1940	57,246	43.5	74,424	56.5
1950	54,230	36.0	96,468	64.0
1960	54,054	30.1	125,269	69.9
1970	53,887	26.5	149,325	73.5
1980	59,495	26.3	167,051	73.7

Sources: Data for 1850–1970 are calculated from *The Historical Statistics of the United States*, Series A 57–72. (Washington, DC: U.S. Department of Commerce, Bureau of the Census, 1985), 11–12. Data for 1980 are calculated from *The Statistical Abstract of the United States: 1984*. (Washington, DC: U.S. Department of Commerce, Bureau of the Census, 1983), 27.
Note: An *urban* area is defined here as an area with a population of 2,500 or more.

families.[7] In addition, attitudes of rural residents differ from the urban population in a variety of ways that will be discussed later in this chapter.[8] Thus, there is clear support for the argument from a neoevolutionary model that the shift from an agricultural to an industrial economy caused major changes in the family situation. To better understand the nature of these changes, it is beneficial to move to a more micro-analytic approach, life-course theory, and cohort analysis.

The Micro-Level

Norman B. Ryder suggests that the concept of cohort is useful both for studying social change (inter-cohort differences) and social diversity (intra-cohort variation).[9] Since the publication of Ryder's article, a number of researchers, particularly in demography, have used cohort analysis to study a wide range of topics. Life-course theory builds on a basic cohort approach, but it suggests that historical events and changes may have differential effects on different cohorts who experience the event at the same time. As noted earlier, Glen H. Elder has applied this approach in looking at the effects of the Depression on families and children, and the model has been used more broadly to examine how economic change affects family life.[10]

Neoevolutionary theory at the macro-level is sometimes criticized for ignoring the complexity of historical change. When it is combined with a life-course approach at a more micro-analytic level, however, the result is a very powerful model for understanding the impact of the broader changes on family life.

One macro-level change, for example, is the dramatic decline in mortality rates in the West over the past two centuries. A neoevolutionary approach would suggest that changes in the environment and changes in technology need to be examined as causal factors in this decline. A lively debate has developed in the literature, which examines the relative effects of medicine, nutrition, public health, and other factors in the mortality decline.[11] None of these authors, however, provides much insight into how the decline had an impact on the everyday lives of families.

Peter Uhlenberg (1980) begins with the mortality data from the macro-level and then applies a life-course approach. He illustrates how the decline in mortality has affected different cohorts of Americans and how its meaning is altered depending on what stage of the individual life course is examined. Thus, given the higher average mortality and fertility rates, Uhlenberg shows that the probability of one or more children in a family dying before the age of fifteen was .62 in 1900, and only .04 by 1976. Likewise, the probability of a child having a member of his or her nuclear family die before he or she reached age fifteen was .51 in 1900, while less than one in ten experienced such a death in 1976. Uhlenberg outlines the implications of mortality shifts for other age groups in each cohort, and thus provides a clear picture of the implications of the broader change for the lives of individuals.[12] Because these shifts in mortality have profound implications for family life, they are the focus of a more complete examination in chapter 4.

This same type of logic must be applied to the analysis of the shift from an agricultural to an industrial economy. In every historical period there are differences between farm and non-farm families. As noted earlier, changes in a whole range of important family varibles over time can be linked with the shift in the proportion of each cohort that is in the agricultural sector. At the same time, researchers cannot assume that farm life meant the same thing for everyone within a cohort or for farmers in different cohorts. A few examples are appropriate to illustrate this point.

Even a cursory reading of tables 3–1 and 3–2 clearly points out that being a farmer in a rural area in 1980 is very different than being a rural farmer in the mid-nineteenth century. A larger percentage of the cohorts alive in 1850 were farmers, and many of their non-farming neighbors still lived in rural settings. The overwhelming majority of the cohorts alive in contemporary society live in urban areas and are in occupations other than farming.

Farming itself has been transformed over the past century, and particularly during the last several decades. The increasing costs of equipment, seed, fertilizers, and land, coupled with little if any increase in prices for crops have moved farming from a small family career to the scale of agribusiness. The size of farms has increased, and the probability of economic success has become less certain.

Careful research that examines the implications of these broader changes for specific cohorts of farm and non-farm families in different historical periods is important for expanding our understanding of social change in families over the past century. The remaining chapters of this book focus on a series of issues related to the shift from an agricultural to an industrial economy and how this has transformed the structure, content, and meaning of family life in our society. The next section of this chapter contrasts farm and non-farm families today as a first step toward developing this broader picture of social change and families.

Intra-Cohort Variation: The Impact of Farm Life on Families

Now that a general model for understanding social change and families in the context of the transition from a rural agricultural society to an urban industrial society has been outlined, it is useful to examine current intra-cohort variation along this dimension. This concluding section of the chapter will review relevant literature that looks at the unique characteristics of farm life, and then will use data from a national sample collected by the National Opinion Research Center (NORC) at the University of Chicago to document differences and similarities between farm and non-farm families.

E. A. Wilkening (1981) argues that "in contrast to most other occupations, farming provides the physical, economic, and social conditions that coincide with the needs, interests, and biological processes of the family."[13] He goes on to say that despite the massive social and cultural changes of the past century, in farming "the family continues to be more closely associated with the productive processes than in most other occupational pursuits." Thus, the separation of work from the home and the development of separate spheres that has been cited as a key result of industrialization do not seem to apply to farm families in the same way as they do to other families. Wilkening suggests that this unique characteristic is responsible for many of the differences that are observed between farm and non-farm families. (The implications of this separation of spheres for changes in the roles of men and women is the topic of a later chapter.)

P. C. Rosenblatt and associates (1978, 1981) describe some of these differences. They agree with Wilkening that the farm family works together at the same economic enterprise. Work and home life are not separated physically, and thus the home cannot be perceived as an escape from the world of work in the same way as it might in other occupations. Because of the linkage to the ownership of land, farming is highly intergenerational. Thus, kinship ties maintain an occupational significance not found in other jobs.[14]

There are further aspects of farming that affect the day-to-day existence of farm families. Income is unpredictable. In contrast to other occupations, personal skills and decisions have less impact on income. Many of the causal factors predicting success or failure (such as political shifts in price supports, weather, and attacks of disease or insects) are beyond the control of individual farmers. Not only are there extreme variations in income, but there are also wide seasonal variations in work requirements of farm family members. On farms that have livestock or dairy cattle, in particular, there is little or no flexibility in the time demands for at least one family member. This limits the time budget of the entire family in ways not experienced by urban families. When this is coupled with the relative physical isolation of farm families, it is clear that interaction patterns differ significantly from urban families.[15]

A careful exploration of the implications of these unique characteristics of farm families is essential. As a first step, data from the NORC General Social Surveys will now be briefly examined to document some of the differences between farm and non-farm families in the contemporary United States.

Since 1972, NORC has interviewed a sample of the adult population in the United States on a wide range of issues using the General Social Survey.[16] The samples are representative of the English-speaking, noninstitutionalized population over the age of eighteen in the United States. Block quota sampling was used in 1972, 1973, 1974, and for half of the 1975 and 1976 surveys. Full probability sampling has been used in subsequent surveys.

The sample size is approximately 1,500 in each year (ranging from 1,468 in 1980 to 1,860 in 1982, with a mean of 1,558). In each year, the percentage of the total sample who list farming as their occupation is near the national average—ranging from 1.6 percent to 3.3 percent, with no trend attributable to any change other than sampling error. The percentages change slightly when those who list a spouse as a farmer are also included, yielding a range of 2.6 percent to 5.8 percent. The largest proportion of these farmers is male (averaged over the years, 86.6 percent are men, 13.4 percent are women) is contrast to other occupations combined, where the distribution is less uneven, and women slightly outnumber men (56.2 percent to 43.8 percent). Racial distributions are nearly identical for farm and non-farm respondents (approximately 86 percent white, 13 percent black, and 1 percent other).

The original plan of analysis was to compare the 1973 and 1983 data to examine trends in the differentials between farm and non-farm respondents. Because there were very few differences between the two years, only the most recent data are presented here. In most cases the *chi* squares of cross-tabulations were not significant because of the extreme disparity in sample sizes between the farm and non-farm respondents. Because of this, most of the discussion of results will be in prose rather than tabular format.[17]

Demographic Variables

Most of the descriptive demographic statistics reflect differentials found in previous research. Farmers (especially women) were more likely to be married than non-farm respondents. There were no differences in age at first marriage, but farm women were less likely to have ever been divorced. The mean age of the farm respondents was older, and they had more children.

Farmers were much less likely to have completed degrees of higher education, and their mean number of years of education was considerably lower for both sexes (44.4 percent of the farm men and 39.1 percent of the farm women had ten or less years of education, while only 19.8 percent of non-farm men and 18.9 percent of non-farm women had this level of education).

The family income for farmers is lower than for the non-farm respondents. They are also less likely to have two adult wage-earners in the home. This is reflected in the respondents' families of orientation as well. There are striking differences in the likelihood that the respondents' mothers worked for pay after they were married. Table 3–3 illustrates that farm men and women were much less likely to have had a mother who worked after she was married, and particularly while she had small children in the home.

In sum, the demographic differences between farm and non-farm respondents were all in the direction that would be predicted from the general model presented earlier in this chapter and from the previous research. They are more likely to be married, have more children, and have lower educational and income levels than non-farm respondents.

Table 3–3

Responses to Questions on the Work Status of Respondent's Mother by Sex and Farm/non-Farm Status: 1983

		Male		Female	
Question	Response	Farm	Non-Farm	Farm	Non-Farm
"Did your mother ever work for pay as long as a year after she was married?"	Yes	30%	62.3%	57.1%	60.1%
	No	70%	37.7%	42.9%	39.9%
		(n=30)	(n=589)	(n=21)	(n=794)
"Did she work for as long as a year before you started first grade?"	Yes	12.5%	44.6%	18.2%	40.8%
	No	87.5%	55.4%	81.8%	59.2%
		(n=8)	(n=350)	(n=11)	(n=453)

Source: Questions and data are drawn from the National Opinion Research Center (NORC) General Social Survey. Information on this data set can be found in James A. Davis, *General Social Surveys, 1972–1984: Cumulative Codebook.* (Chicago: National Opinion Research Center, 1983).

Farm women are less likely to work for pay after marriage, but this difference was much more pronounced in their parents' generation.

Attitudinal Variables

In contrast to the consistent predictability of differences in demographic variables, attitudinal differences between the farm and nonfarm respondents were much more complex. Consistent with previous research, farmers had higher rates of attendance at religious services, and this tendency for a higher religiosity (as measured by attendance) did correspond with some of the attitude differences. Farm respondents were more likely to define premarital sex as morally wrong, although there was little difference between the farm and non-farm respondents in their estimations of the morality of extramarital and homosexual behavior. (In the 1973 sample the result was the opposite—the two groups did not differ on premarital sexual attitudes, but farmers were more likely to label both homosexual and extramarital sexual behavior as morally wrong.)

The differences in attitudes on abortion are both more complex and more interesting. Both groups overwhelmingly support legal abortion in cases in which the mother's health is in danger (approximately 90 percent). There are also only small differences in the proportion supporting legal abortion in cases in which the mother is poor. The differences that do emerge appear either to be gender-based or to reflect an interaction between gender and the farm/non-farm dichotomy. Women in both groups are more likely to approve of legal abortion in cases in which there is a chance of serious birth defect and farm women are most likely to approve when the pregnancy is a result of rape. It is non-farm men who are more likely to approve of legal abortion when a woman is single and does not want to marry the man. (For more on historical shifts in attitudes about sexuality in the general population, see chapter 8.)

These simple comparisons are not meant as an adequate description of how farm families and individuals differ from the rest of the population. They are illustrative, however, of the lines of inquiry that deserve more careful scrutiny in the future. They also provide further support for the idea that a key to understanding why and how American families have been transformed over the past century is the fact that we have moved from a nation of rural farm families to an urban industrial society.

This chapter has argued that the complex set of changes in family variables over the last century can best be understood when placed in the context of the broader shift from an agricultural to an industrial economy. The model presented suggests that linking neoevolutionary theory at the macro-level with life-course theory and cohort analysis at the micro-level will help expand our understanding of this transition in family life and its impact on individuals in different cohorts.

National data were used to document the decreasing proportions of the population employed in the agricultural sector as well as the decreasing proportions of the population living in rural areas. These broader trends make it clear that the meaning and experience of being a rural farm family has been different for various cohorts. Not only have they moved from being a majority of each cohort to a small minority, but the technological and economic changes that shape the realities of farm life have transformed it from a small family enterprise to a large business venture.

Nonetheless, we have seen that farm families are substantially different than non-farm families because of the nature of farming. Its demands on time, the uncontrollable nature of important factors such as weather, prices and crop success, the relative isolation of farm families, and the key importance of land ownership and transfer all have direct and indirect implications for the structure and process of farm families.

Data from the NORC General Social Surveys were used to give a few brief illustrations of some differences between farm and non-farm repondents on a number demographic and attitudinal variables. Farmers have higher marriage and fertility rates, lower divorce rates, and more conservative moral values on family issues, but the linkages between farm life and variation in these characteristics are complex. Further research must begin to examine the structuring of these linkages in different cohorts of farmers as well as within cohorts of the farm population to expand our understanding of how the broader transformation from an agricultural to an industrial society has transformed family life.

This chapter began by asking the broad question, "How have families in the United States *actually* been changing?" This is the organizing question throughout the rest of the book, but in the context of this chapter, the answer to the question is: *Families in the United States have been transformed over the last century as they have become more urban and as they have moved from farm to non-farm occupations.*

This broad transformation of technological level has many implications beyond the direct effects of the type of employment people have or whether or not they live in rural areas. Central to the change has been the transformation of birth and death. The next chapter focuses on some of these changes and their implications for the lives of individuals and families.

Notes

1. William J. Goode, *The Family*, 2nd ed. (Englewood Cliffs, NJ: Prentice-Hall, 1982).

2. This phrase is drawn from the title of one of the classic works in historical demography, Peter Laslett's *The World We Have Lost* (New York: Charles Scribner's Sons, 1965). A central argument of this book is that many aspects of family life before industrialization (such as the nuclear family as the basic domestic group) were much more like families today than we realize.

3. Many authors have focused on this shift. One of the clearest statements of some of its implications is found in Barbara Laslett's "The Family as a Public and Private Institution: An Historical Perspective," *Journal of Marriage and the Family*, 22 (1973):480–592.

4. See U.S. Bureau of the Census, "Marital Status and Living Arrangements: March 1979," *Current Population Reports* (1980) Series P–20, No. 349, and R. S. Miller "Role Transitions of Professionals Moving to Rural Locales," in V. L. Allen and E. van de Vliert (eds.), *Role Transitions* (New York: Plenum Press, 1984), pp. 213–226.

5. See R. L. Bushman, "Family Security in the Transition from Farm to City, 1750–1850," *Journal of Family History*, (Fall 1981):238–255.

6. See J. Q. Graham, Jr., "Family and Fertility in Rural Ohio: Wood County, Ohio in 1860," *Journal of Family History* 8(3):262–278, 1983; A. M. Guest and S. E. Tolnay, "Children's Roles and Fertility: Late Nineteenth-Century United States," *Social Science History* 7(4):355–380, 1983.

7. See D. L. Brown, "A Quarter Century of Trends and Changes in the Demographic Structure of American Families," in R. T. Coward and W. M. Smith, Jr. (eds.), *The Family in Rural Society* (Boulder, CO: Westview Press, 1981), pp. 9–25.

8. More complete discussions of attitude differences between rural and urban families can be found in O. F. Larson, "Values and Beliefs of Rural People," pp 91–112, in the book cited in note 7; Norval D. Glenn and L. Hill, Jr., "Rural-Urban Differences in Attitudes and Behavior in the United States," *Annals, AAPSS* 429 (1977):36–50; and Edward L. Kain and Diana J. Divecha "Rural Women's Attitudes Toward Social Change in Work and Family Roles," a paper presented at the 1983 annual meetings of the National Council on Family Relations.

9. Norman B. Ryder, "The Cohort as a Concept in the Study of Social Change," *American Sociological Review* 30 (1965):843–861.

10. See Glen H. Elder, Jr., *Children of the Great Depression: Social Change in Life Experience* (Chicago: The University of Chicago Press, 1974); and Phyllis Moen, Edward L. Kain, and Glen H. Elder, Jr., "Economic Conditions and Family Life: Contemporary and Historical Perspectives," in Richard Nelson and Felicity Skidmore (eds.), *American Families and the Economy: The High Costs of Living* (Washington, DC: National Academy Press, 1983), pp. 213–254.

11. See, for example, T. McKeown, "Medicine and World Population," in M. Sheps and J. Ridley (eds.), *Public Health and Population Change* (Pittsburgh: University of Pittsburgh Press, 1965), pp. 25–40; T. McKeown, "Medical Issues in Historical Demography," in Edwin Clarke (ed.), *Modern Methods in the History of Medicine* (London, 1971), pp. 57–74; T. McKeown, R. G. Brown and R. G. Record, "An Interpretation of the Modern Rise of Population in Europe," *Population Studies* 26(3):345–382, 1972; T. McKeown, R. G. Record, and R. D. Turner, "An Interpretation of the Decline of Mortality in England and Wales During the Twentieth Century," *Population Studies* 29(3):391–422, 1975; P. E. Razzell, "An Interpretation of the Modern Rise of Population in Europe"—A Critique," *Population Studies* 28(1):5–17, 1974; S. H. Preston, "The Changing Relation Between Mortality and Level of Economic Development," *Population Studies* 29(2):231–248, 1975; and E. A. Wrigley, *Population and History* (New York: McGraw-Hill, 1969).

12. See Peter Uhlenberg, "Death and the Family," *Journal of Family History* 5(3): 313–320, 1980.

13. See E. A. Wilkening, "Farm Families and Family Farming," in R. T. Coward and W. Smith Jr. (eds.), *The Family in Rural Society* (Boulder, CO: Westview Press, Inc., 1981).

14. See P. C. Rosenblatt, A. Nevaldine, and S. L. Titus, "Farm Families: Relation of Significant Attributes of Farming to Family Interaction," *International Journal of Sociology* 8 (1978):89–99; P. C. Rosenblatt and R. M. Anderson, "Interaction in Farm Families: Tension and Stress," in R. T. Coward and W. Smith, Jr. (eds.), *The Family in Rural Society* (Boulder, CO: Westview Press, Inc., 1981).

15. I am indebted to Ms. Joan Doughty for her background work on farm families in the United States, which provided information for this section of the chapter.

16. See James A. Davis, Principal Investigator; Tom W. Smith, Senior Study Director, *General Social Surveys, 1972–1983* (Machine-readable data file) (NORC ed., Chicago: National Opinion Research Center, producer, 1983, Storrs, CT: Roper Public Opinion Research Center, University of CT, distributor).

17. Fuller descriptions of the data can be obtained by consulting "The American Transition from an Agricultural to an Industrial Economy and its Effect on Family Life," a paper I presented at the 1984 meetings of the National Council on Family Relations in San Francisco. This paper formed the foundation of the current chapter.

4
Until Death Do Us Part

As the productive base of this country was transformed from a rural farm economy to an urban industrial economy, the demography of family life underwent changes that were no less radical. During successive decades, families had fewer and fewer children, and each cohort of children had better chances of survival than those born previously.

Most people realize that American families have fewer children today than in the past, and that these children are more likely to survive to adulthood, but the implications of these changes are seldom fully appreciated. This chapter looks at these two demographic changes—the declines in fertility and mortality—and explores some of the impacts they have had on family life in this country over the last century.

The Demographic Transition—
a Macro-Analytic Perspective

On a worldwide scale, the declines in fertility and mortality have been labelled the demographic transition. In most Western industrial countries, declines in mortality began first, as advances in medicine, public health, and nutrition significantly reduced the chances of death, particularly among infants. Birth rates remained high, and thus populations increased at a rapid rate. This difference between birth and death rates continues to be the cause of population problems in many Third World countries today, and the politics of birth control programs are hotly debated throughout the world.[1] Declines in fertility rates came later, and only when the reduction in family size reached a significant level did the growth in population slow to the extent that relative stability was again reached in the West. This imbalance between birth and death rates is not a new phenomenon. At many points throughout history, there have been famines or epidemics (such as the Black Death in Europe), which have increased the mortality rate to such an extent that the size of the population significantly declined. Recent centuries, however, have been characterized by population growth. It is only in the twentieth century that this growth has reached such magnitude that the very survival of the human species is threatened.[2]

An entire volume could be dedicated to a description and analysis of the worldwide demographic transition of the past century. In this chapter, however, the focus will be on declines in fertility and mortality in the United States and their implications for family life. Because many authors have examined the declines in fertility elsewhere, I will only briefly review some of the basic information here, and the emphasis throughout the rest of the chapter will be on the impact of mortality declines on family life over the past century.

Fewer Babies, Smaller Households

If we could step back and look at a list of all of the changes that have happened to families over the past century in this country, it is likely that one of the most striking changes on the list would be the decline in the average household size.

Table 4–1 illustrates the dramatic decline in average household size since the founding of this country. In 1790, over one-third of U.S. households contained seven or more individuals, a striking contrast to the typical household of today. The number of people who live together in a household in the late twentieth century is much smaller than the number living together even at the turn of the century.

In 1900, over one-fifth of the households in this country included seven or more people. Only three decades later, scarcely one in ten households had seven or more individuals, and the most common household type included only two members. By 1985, over half the households in the United States had only one or two members, and only about 1 percent had seven or more. (See table 4–1.)

It is important to note that I am using the term *household* here rather than family. Most of the national data in this country are collected on sets of individuals who share a residence. While in many instances this household unit is also a family, this is not always the case. The household may consist of unrelated individuals, it may include a family plus additional members who are either related or unrelated to the family, or it may be an individual living alone.

The decline in household size throughout this time period certainly reflects a decline in family size. Families are having fewer children now

Table 4–1
Percentages of Different Household Sizes: Selected Years, 1790–1985

Number in Household	1790	1900	1930	1960	1985
1	3.7%	5.1%	7.9%	13.1%	23.7%
2	7.8	15.0	23.4	27.8	31.6
3	11.7	17.6	20.8	18.9	17.8
4	13.8	16.9	17.5	17.6	15.7
5	13.9	14.2	12.0	11.5	7.0
6	13.2	10.9	7.6	5.7	2.6
7+	35.8	20.4	10.9	5.4	1.5

Sources: Data for 1790–1960 are from *The Historical Statistics of the United States*, Series A 335–349. (Washington, DC: U.S. Department of Commerce, Bureau of the Census, 1985), 42. Data for 1984 are from *The Statistical Abstract of the United States: 1987*. (Washington, DC: U.S. Department of Commerce, Bureau of the Census, 1986), 45, Table 59.

than they did in the past. In 1800, there were 278 children born per 1,000 white women between the ages of fifteen and forty-four, meaning that more than one out of every four women in the childbearing years had a child that year alone. By 1984, that rate had fallen to 62.2 per 1,000 for white women—a decline to approximately one birth per seventeen women in the childbearing years.

Declines in fertility were relatively continuous throughout the eighteenth, nineteenth, and early twentieth centuries, until the baby boom of the 1940s and 1950s. It is important to note that throughout all of this time the fertility rate of black families was considerably higher than that of white families. The first comparable data are found in 1920, and at that point in time, the fertility rate for women in the childbearing years was 137.5 for black women, compared to 115.4 for white women. By 1984, the rate for white women had dropped to 62.2 births per 1,000 women and the rate for black women had fallen to 81.4 births per 1,000 women.[3] This contrast points to the fact that differences within a cohort (intra-cohort variation) are important considerations when talking about family change. Most of the data reviewed in this book combine information from diverse groups within a cohort, and this can sometimes mask important differences within the population. These differences will be the focus of the analysis of mortality change presented in the second section of this chapter.[4]

While there is no doubt that typical American families have become smaller over the past several centuries, the shifts in household size since the turn of this century also reflect several other trends in household composition. Most importantly, since 1900, there has been a significant decline in the number of non-family members in the household. In the nineteenth century it was a common adaptive strategy, particularly for urban households, to take in boarders and lodgers to supplement the family income.[5] Many families also had domestic servants who lived in their home. This practice declined throughout the late nineteenth century and virtually disappeared with the onset of the Great Depression. (More mention will be made of domestic servants in chapter 6, when female labor-force participation is examined.)

Another change causing a reduction in household size is the decline of non-nuclear family members sharing a household with their kin. In the past, unmarried relatives, for example, were much more likely to live with the family of a kin member. Today these people are likely to live by themselves, contributing to the drastic increase of one-person households since the turn of the century. Similarly, in the past, if a family could not afford to care for all of its children, a common practice was for one or more of the children to live in the household of a relative. This pattern has also declined over time.

Just as with the patterns of fertility, however, the structuring of households has varied considerably by race. Historically, black families have been much more likely to have households that included members from more than one nuclear family, and it is still the case today that blacks are more likely than whites to live in households with their relatives. In 1985, for example, only 6.6 percent of white men between the ages of twenty-five and sixty-four and 12.6 percent of white women in the same age group were living in households of relatives other than their spouse. For the black population, the figures were 13.7 percent and 35 percent, respectively. Indeed, throughout the adult years, blacks are about twice as likely as whites to share a household with relatives other than their spouse.[6]

The implications of these changes in fertility and household size for everyday life within the family are enormous. Perhaps the most important result has been an increase in family and individual privacy. Barbara Laslett (1973) has convincingly argued that as the number of children in families and the number of non-nuclear family members in households have declined, individual privacy and freedom have increased. She also suggests that "to the extent that family privacy has increased, . . . it is also likely that there has been a decrease in social control over and social support for a traditional definition of the performance of family roles."[7] This change in traditional roles is a topic explored in more depth in chapter 6.

This increase in family and individual privacy is not something to be taken lightly. Indeed, it may be linked to many other changes that we see in family life throughout this century, including family violence, drug and alcohol abuse, and changes in sexual attitudes and behavior.

As an illustration, think about the simple example of fertility within the family. The typical Colonial family had eight or more children. The typical Colonial house was one large room. (Most families of the era did not reside in the sprawling plantation mansions that have survived to the present day.) A father and mother contemplating having their ninth child did not have the privacy of their own bedroom in which to share their intimacies. While sex may not have been a spectator sport, it is likely that the first eight children had some sense of what was going on between their parents in the other part of the room. While we may lament how early children of the 1980s learn about sex, this is a situation quite foreign to most prospective parents in the latter decades of the twentieth century!

Thus we can see that change in one variable, the size of the typical household, has implications for many aspects of family life. Certainly the decline in fertility has been one of the most important changes occurring in families over the past several hundred years.

No less important is the revolutionary decline in mortality, which has transformed family life. The remainder of this chapter will focus on this second demographic change in families since the turn of the century.[8]

Race, Mortality, and Families

At the turn of the century, orphanhood was a common event, and death touched nuclear families much more often than today. In 1900, infant mortality was ten times its current rate, and maternal mortality was over eighty times the current level. The expectation of life at birth has increased from less than fifty years to nearly seventy-five years. While these changes have had a tremendous impact on both individual development and family life, very little research has focused on the importance of mortality shifts in understanding social change and families in the United States.[9]

The remainder of this chapter examines these mortality changes in three different ways. First, several measures of mortality in three cohorts separated by forty years (1900, 1940, and 1980) are compared to illustrate social change in mortality. Race and sex differences are highlighted to point to the importance of understanding diversity within cohorts as well as between cohorts. Second, variation by race, gender, and ordinal position of children is explored to illustrate how the early life-course experience of Americans has been differentially affected by death. Third, several aspects of later periods in the life course are examined to point to the continued impact of race and gender as variables that modify the implications of mortality change upon the lives of individuals within families.

Summary demographic measures of mortality, such as the expectation of life at birth and age- or group-specific mortality rates are useful for illustrating trends in the overall patterning of mortality. These population statistics do not, however, illuminate the implications of changing mortality for family life. Using a life-course framework, Peter Uhlenberg (1980) has helped to illustrate the profound changes that have occurred in families because of these shifts. His data were calculated comparing three cohorts in the white population: 1900, 1940, and 1976. His analyses suggest the impact of changing mortality on several stages of the life course: childhood, young adulthood, middle age, and old age. This section of the chapter starts with the foundation laid by Uhlenberg and examines how race and sex differences in mortality rates have had an impact on the early life-course experience of black and white families since the turn of the century. In particular, this discussion focuses on the lives of children. While Uhlenberg's emphasis was on inter-cohort variation, this chapter focuses on intra-cohort variation, and points to the importance of race, gender, and ordinal position in modifying the impact of change in mortality on the early life-course experience of individuals within the family. Several illustrations are also provided that examine the impact of within-cohort mortality differences on later stages of the life course.

The discussion is divided into three parts that correspond to three interrelated questions. The first section asks the question, "Why should we be interested in intra-cohort differences in mortality?" Several measures of mortality are compared in three cohorts to illustrate the large variation within cohort by both race and gender. The second section uses a life-course framework to illustrate the impact of some of these mortality changes on the lives of children, and how the variables of race, sex, and ordinal position predict very different experiences of mortality for children in families. The final section provides some brief suggestions about intra-cohort variation in the experiences of mortality in other stages of the life course, and summarizes some of the intra-cohort variations in mortality and its impact on family life.

Why Should We Be Interested in Intra-Cohort Differences in Mortality?

Norman B. Ryder (1965) suggests that inter-cohort comparisons can help us to understand social change and intra-cohort comparisons can help illuminate diversity *within* a cohort.[10] Since the turn of the century, mortality rates have drastically declined in the United States. This is true in every measure of mortality—from infant and maternal mortality rates to expectation of life at birth. In each cohort, however, race and sex differences are evident. The race differences at the turn of the century painted

Table 4–2
Expectation of Life at Birth by Race and Sex: 1900, 1940, and 1980

Year	White		Black and Other	
	Male	*Female*	*Male*	*Female*
1900	48.2	51.1	32.5	35.0
1940	62.8	67.3	52.3	55.5
1980	70.7	78.1	63.7	72.3

Sources: Data for 1900 and 1940 are from *The Historical Statistics of the United States* (Washington, DC: U.S. Department of Commerce, Bureau of the Census, 1985).

strikingly different pictures for the life chances of blacks and whites. (See table 4–2.) In 1990, for example, the expectation of life at birth was 48.2 for white men and 51.1 for white women. The corresponding figures for the black population were 32.5 and 35, respectively. By 1980, whites continued to have a longer life expectation, but the race difference was now approximately six years, compared with sixteen years at the turn of the century. (See table 4–3.)

An examination of tables 4–2 and 4–3 clearly illustrates that both race and gender are important variables in predicting mortality rates throughout this century. In all three cohorts, the expectation of life at birth is higher for whites than for non-whites, and within racial group, it is higher for women than for men.[11] Table 4–3 illustrates, however, that the historical trends in race and sex differences are moving in opposite directions. This difference merits further explanation.

Historical Changes in Sex Differences in Mortality. Within racial group, the sex difference in expectation of life at birth has been increasing. A

Table 4–3
Race and Sex Differences in the Expectation of Life at Birth: 1900, 1940, and 1980

Year	Sex Difference (F–M)		Race Difference (W–B&O)	
	White	*Black and Other*	*Male*	*Female*
1900	2.9	2.5	15.7	16.1
1940	4.5	3.2	10.5	11.8
1980	7.4	8.6	7	5.8

Sources: Data for 1900 and 1940 are from *The Historical Statistics of the United States* (Washington, DC: U.S. Department of Commerce, Bureau of the Census, 1985). Data for 1980 are from *The Statistical Abstract of the United States, 1986* (Washington, DC: U.S. Department of Commerce, Bureau of the Census, 1986).

major explanation of this trend is the dramatic decline in maternal mortality rates since the turn of the century. From the point of conception, men have a higher age-specific mortality rate than women. While the sex ratio (the number of men per one hundred women) is approximately 124 at conception, it drops to about 104 for full-term births.[12] At birth, most societies report a slight excess of boys over girls, but by adulthood, women outnumber men, and current cross-national data indicate that the life expectation at birth is higher for women than men in virtually every society worldwide in spite of extremely high maternal mortality rates in some cultures.[13] As a result, when maternal mortality begins to decline, the sex difference in life expectation at birth increases over time.

Table 4–4 illustrates the decline in maternal mortality rates in the United States by comparing three different cohorts.[14] While the maternal mortality rate has declined in both racial groups, the table illustrates that the race differences have actually increased over time. In 1915, non-white groups had a rate that was 1.76 times that of whites. By 1980, this ratio had increased to 2.86. The most plausible explanation for this increase is that the medical technology and services that have been responsible for the precipitous decline in maternal mortality are more available to white women because of social class (particularly income) disparities between racial groups in our society. A considerable number of developed countries have maternal and infant mortality rates that are lower than the United States, and this is often attributed to the lack of national programs in the United States supporting children and families. Programs and policies that provide for things as varied as childcare services, maternity and paternity leave, sick leave to parents when a child is ill, and medical benefits for mothers and children regardless of income are sadly lacking in the United States compared with many other industrialized countries.[15]

Table 4–4
Race Differences in Maternal and Infant Mortality Rates: 1915, 1940, and 1980

Year	Maternal Mortality Rate (deaths per 10,000 live births)			Infant Mortality Rate (deaths per 1,000 live births)		
	White	Black & Other	B&O/W	White	Black & Other	B&O/W
1900	60.1	105.6	1.76	98.6	181.2	1.84
1940	32.0	77.4	2.42	43.2	73.8	1.71
1980	.7	2	2.86	11.1	19.1	1.72

Sources: Data for 1915 and 1940 are from *The Historical Statistics of the United States* (Washington, DC: U.S. Department of Commerce, Bureau of the Census, 1985). Data for 1980 are from *The Statistical Abstract of the United States, 1986* (Washington, DC: U.S. Department of Commerce, Bureau of the Census, 1986).

Historical Changes in Race Differences in Mortality. Social class differences (in access to medical services, nutrition, adequate housing, etc.) are likely the major reason for the persistence in race differences in expectation of life at birth that are evident in table 4–3. The three cohorts compared at forty-year intervals illustrate that the race difference has declined over time for both men and women. In 1900, white women and men outlived black women and men by about 16 years. By 1980, the advantage of whites over blacks had declined to 7 years for men and 5.8 years for women. This change is a result of a combination of declines in various age-specific measures of mortality.

As table 4–4 illustrates, however, changes have not always occurred at the same rates for blacks and whites. While the maternal mortality rate has declined faster for whites than blacks, this is not true of the infant mortality rate. Table 4–4 illustrates that the ratio of the non-white to white infant mortality rate has remained relatively constant throughout the century. Thus, while infant mortality rates are one-tenth the magnitude they were in 1915, the white infant mortality rate is still about half that of other racial groups.

Summary measures of mortality clearly illustrate the importance of race and gender as predictors of variation within a cohort. They do not, however, provide a very clear picture of how the change in mortality rates has affected the lives of individuals. The next section of the chapter takes a closer look at the implications of intra-cohort and inter-cohort variation in mortality on one stage of the life course—childhood.

*What Are the Implications of Intra-Cohort Differences
in Mortality for Childhood?*

Uhlenberg (1980) used life table values to calculate the probabilities of different mortality-related events (such as orphanhood and loss of spouse) occurring in various cohorts. The methods from this earlier paper are used here to examine three types of intra-cohort differences in the life-course experience of children. The Uhlenberg paper clearly illustrates the massive impact of mortality change on family life during this century. This impact has varied considerably, however, between groups within each cohort. Here I will use the variables of race, sex, and ordinal position to illustrate some of this variation.

Life Chances During Childhood. In preindustrial societies, the periods of highest age-specific mortality are during infancy and childhood. As nutrition, sanitation, and medical technology are developed so that their combined effect limits the number of infant deaths during childbirth and due to early childhood diseases, the chances of survival to adulthood are radically altered. Many of these changes began throughout the eighteenth and nineteenth centuries in the United States, yet the rapid rate of decline in infant and childhood mortality continued well into the twentieth century. Table 4–5 illustrates that the probability of survival for the 1900 cohort was considerably less than for cohorts later in the century.

Just as striking are the race and sex differences in the probability of a child surviving to adolescence. To take the extreme example, in 1900, the probabilities of a black boy surviving to adolescence were slightly better than three out of five. In contrast, a white girl's chances of survival were better than four out of five. When inter-cohort and intra-cohort differences are compared, the difference between blacks and whites in 1900 is as large as the forty year difference between white cohorts from 1900 to 1940.

The Loss of a Sibling. Another way to think about how variation in mortality affects the lives of children is to examine the probability that a child will have one or more siblings die. Table 4–6 uses differential mortality rates to contrast the probabilities of loss of a sibling if we assume that the child has two siblings—one of whom is a sister, and one of whom is a brother. This assumption results in an *underestimate* of both social change and social diversity because of the patterning of fertility over time and by race.

Since the turn of the century, the total completed fertility of women in this country has dropped from over four to less than two children. As noted in the first section of this chapter, blacks have had a higher fertility rate than whites throughout the period. Thus, a child in 1900 would be

Table 4–5

Race and Sex Differences in the Probability of Children Surviving to Age Fifteen: 1900, 1940, and 1978

	White		Black & Other	
Year	Male	Female	Male	Female
1900	.78	.83	.64	.68
1940	.93	.95	.90	.92
1978	.98	.99	.97	.98

Source: Probabilities are calculated from life table values in *Vital Statistics of the United States: 1978*, Vol. II, Part A. (Washington, DC: DHHS Pub. No. 83–1101, Government Printing Office, 1982), Table 5–4.

Note: Data for 1900 are for death registration states and include only blacks in the "black and other" category.

Data for 1940 and 1978 are for the complete population.

Blacks always comprise at least 95 percent of the "black and other" group.

Table 4–6
Race Differences in the Probability of Death of One or More of Two Siblings Before a Child Reaches Age Fifteen: 1900, 1940, and 1978

Year	White	Black and Other	B&O/W
1900	.35	.56	1.6
1940	.12	.17	1.4
1978	.03	.05	1.7

Source: Probabilities are calculated from life table values in *Vital Statistics of the United States: 1978*, Vol. II, Part A. (Washington, DC: DHHS Pub. No. 83–1101, Government Printing Office, 1982), Table 5–4.

Note: This table assumes that the child has two siblings—one sister and one brother. As a result, it *underestimates* the rates for non-whites relative to whites, and the rates of earlier cohorts versus later cohorts, given differential fertility between races and between cohorts.

Data for 1900 are for death registration states, and include only blacks in the "black and other" category.

Data for 1940 and 1978 are for the complete population.

Blacks always comprise at least 95 percent of the "black and other" group.

likely to have *more* than two siblings (resulting in an underestimate of his or her probabilities of losing a sibling to death), and a child in 1978 would be likely to have *less* than two siblings (resulting in an overestimate of his or her probabilities of losing a sibling to death). Similarly, within each cohort, a black child would, on the average, have more siblings than a white child, thus underestimating the race difference in the probabilities of losing a sibling to death. Throughout this chapter, the estimates that are derived are conservative estimates of both inter-cohort and intra-cohort differences. They are meant to illustrate the diversity of experience when only one variable—mortality—is examined. Other variables, such as fertility, rather than moderating the effects of mortality, tend to accentuate the differences. This will be discussed in the final section of the chapter.

Race is clearly a powerful factor in predicting whether or not a child is likely to have one of his or her siblings die. In all three cohorts, black children are about one and a half times as likely as white children to have this experience. In 1900, the chances were about one in three that a white child would lose a sibling before reaching age fifteen. For black children, the probability of this event was over one in two. For both racial groups, the experience is much less likely today—with the chances being only three in one hundred and five in one hundred for whites and blacks, respectively.

The Incidence of Orphanhood. While the loss of a sibling may have implications for children in terms of household responsibilities, the number of people within the household with whom affection, food, and other resources must be shared, and the emotional trauma of death, it is clear that the death of a parent is far more significant. Social insurance was unknown in 1900, and the death of either parent, particularly the father, could mean an overnight move from relative financial security into destitution. If the child was older when the event occurred, an unplanned transition into adulthood and the status of household head, or at least major breadwinner, could be one result of orphanhood.

Table 4–7 presents the probability of a child losing one, either, or both parents. The first column indicates the probability of the child's father dying before the child reaches age fifteen. The next three columns illustrate the probabilities of losing a mother, the probabilities of losing either parent, and finally, the chances of losing both parents before the child reaches age fifteen. Again, we see that within each cohort, black children are much more likely to have a parent die than white children. In the 1900 cohort, for example, the chances are about one in five that during childhood, a black child will lose his or her father. The probability of this happening for a white child is closer to one in ten. The chances are one in three that a black child who is born when both parents are age twenty-five will lose one or other parent. Black children in this cohort are three times as likely to lose both parents than their white counterparts. In the 1940 and 1978 cohorts, the race difference in this final column is accentuated. Black children are about ten times as likely to lose both parents before they reach the age of fifteen.

A comparison of the between-cohort variation is again instructive in thinking about the importance of race as a factor in how children experience mortality. The probabilities in all four columns have a striking pat-

Table 4–7

Race Differences in the Probability of an Earlier-Born Child Being Orphaned Before Age Fifteen: 1900, 1940, and 1978

Year	Probability of Father Dying		Probability of Mother Dying		Probability of Either Parent Dying		Probability of Both Parents Dying	
	White	B&O	White	B&O	White	B&O	White	B&O
1900	.12	.19	.11	.17	.22	.33	.01	.03
1940	.05	.13	.04	.12	.09	.23	.002	.02
1978	.03	.06	.01	.03	.04	.09	.0003	.002

Source: Probabilities are calculated from life value tables in *Vital Statistics of the United States: 1978*, Vol. II, Part A. (Washington, DC: DHSS Pub. No. 83–1101, Government Printing Office, 1982), Table 5–4.

Note: This table assumes that the child is born when both parents are age twenty-five, and is thus an earlier-born child.

tern in which the chances of black children being orphaned are forty years behind those of white children. While mortality is declining for both race groups, because of the continuing mortality differential, the rates for blacks in the 1940 cohort match those of whites in the 1900 cohort, and the rates for blacks in 1978 match those of whites in 1940.

The Importance of Ordinal Position. Table 4–7 illustrated the probabilities of orphanhood when it is assumed that the child is born early in the reproductive years of the parents (at age twenty-five for both parents). The ordinal position of the child clearly plays a role, however, in a society in which life expectation is shorter and in which the end of life overlaps with the years of childbearing and childrearing. Later-born children are much more likely to experience orphanhood. This is illustrated in table 4–8, which mirrors the previous table, but assumes instead that the child is born when both parents are age thirty-five. The contrast between these two tables gives a conservative estimate of the importance of ordinal position, since the reproductive years of parents (particularly in cohorts around the turn of the century) usually begin before age twenty-five, and usually end after age thirty-five. Nonetheless, the contrast between tables 4–7 and 4–8 is quite striking. Here we find that black children who are later-born have a one in four chance of losing their father and a one in four chance of losing their mother while they are still in childhood. The probability of losing one or the other is over two in five, and the chances are greater than one in twenty that a black child will have both parents die before the child reaches age fifteen. As with earlier tables, the probabilities of orphanhood are much lower for white children in all three

Table 4–8
Race Differences in the Probability of a Later-Born Child Being
Orphaned Before Age Fifteen: 1900, 1940, and 1978

Year	Probability of Father Dying		Probability of Mother Dying		Probability of Either Parent Dying		Probability of Both Parents Dying	
	White	B&O	White	B&O	White	B&O	White	B&O
1900	.16	.25	.14	.24	.28	.43	.02	.06
1940	.09	.21	.07	.19	.15	.36	.006	.04
1978	.05	.11	.03	.06	.08	.16	.002	.007

Source: Probabilities are calculated from life value tables in *Vital Statistics of the United States: 1978*, Vol. II, Part A. (Washington, DC: DHSS Pub. No. 83–1101, Government Printing Office, 1982), Table 5–4.
Note: This table assumes that the child is born when both parents are age thirty-five, and is thus a later-born child.

cohorts, and again there is a striking similarity in the probabilities by race if we compare the black rates to those we find for whites forty years earlier.

Loss of a Member of the Immediate Nuclear Family. It is clear from these data that successive cohorts of children have had radically different experiences of mortality in terms of the loss of siblings or parents. Further, these experiences vary considerably by race, with white children being much less likely to have a sibling or a parent die. Table 4–9 combines the information from previous tables and asks the question, "What are the chances of having either a sibling or a parent die while you are a child?" Again, we are assuming the child has two siblings—one sister and one brother. The first two columns assume that the child is born when both parents are age twenty-five, and is thus an earlier-born child, and the second two columns assume that the child is later-born, with birth occurring when both parents are age thirty-five. In the latter case, we find that the probabilities of a black child experiencing the death of a nuclear family member were three in four for the 1900 cohort. Remember, that this *underestimates* the probability of that occurrence because completed fertility rates for both blacks and whites were higher than three in 1900. In 1978, black children are twice as likely as white children to have a member of their nuclear family die while they are still in childhood, and later born children are about one and a half times as likely to have a nuclear family member die while they are children. The 1978 estimate of one in five black children losing a nuclear family member to death also is a biased estimate because of the assumption of a completed fertility rate of three.

Table 4–9
Race Differences in the Probability of Death to a Nuclear Family Member Before a Child Reaches Age Fifteen: 1900, 1940, and 1978

	Probability of Death to a Nuclear Family Member if Child Is Born When Both Parents Are Age Twenty-Five		Probability of Death to a Nuclear Family Member if Child Is Born When Both Parents Are Age Thirty-Five	
Year	White	Black & Other	White	Black & Other
1900	.49	.70	.53	.75
1940	.20	.36	.25	.47
1978	.07	.13	.11	.20

Source: Probabilities are calculated from life value tables in *Vital Statistics of the United States: 1978*, Vol. II, Part A. (Washington, DC: DHSS Pub. No. 83–1101, Government Printing Office, 1982), Table 5–4.

Note: This table assumes that the child has one brother and one sister.

When we look at the impact of mortality on family life, all the measures point to the importance of an examination of not only between cohort differences but also a careful examination of within cohort differences, using such variables as race, gender, and ordinal position.

These three variables by no means exhaust the variables of importance. Clearly the experience of black or white children varies by social class as well as by such factors as region and residence. The relationship between variables has changed over time as well. In early cohorts, mortality rates were higher in urban areas because of crowding and poor sanitation. In more recent cohorts, rates for many types of mortality are higher in rural areas, where access to sophisticated medical technology is limited. The importance of some of these other variables is briefly discussed in the concluding section of this chapter. First, however, it is instructive to move beyond childhood and to look at a few examples of intra-cohort variation in the impact of mortality on other stages of the life course.

What Are the Implications of These Intra-Cohort Differences in Mortality for Other Stages of the Life Course and for Family Life in General?

Uhlenberg (1980) moves beyond childhood and clearly illustrates the impact of mortality decline on other stages in the life course. This chapter has kept its major focus on childhood in an attempt to look at the importance of variations within cohorts (social diversity) as well as between cohorts (social change). This concluding section briefly notes some of the implications of intra-cohort variation in mortality for these later stages of the life course, and then closes with a review of some of the major issues raised by an analysis that includes examination of intra-cohort variation in the experience of mortality.

Early Adulthood and Marriage. Variation in mortality within a cohort has a variety of impacts upon decisions about life-course transitions in early adulthood. As noted above, if a child is orphaned, the transition to adulthood may happen at an earlier age as entry into the labor force becomes a necessity. Glen H. Elder (1974) has illustrated that historical events such as the Great Depression also may operate to speed up the assumption of adult responsibilities and may have implications for educational attainment and other activities that take place in early adulthood.[16] The number of people in the marriage market is also affected by mortality shifts and historical events. During the time of a war, an imbalance in the sex ratio that leaves fewer men per one hundred women alters the availability of spouses. Sex differences in mortality from any cause may have an impact on the marital chances of a cohort completely separate from the needs and desires of the individuals in that cohort. (It is currently the case, for example, that during the marriageable years there is an extreme imbalance in the sex ratio among blacks in this country.) One must note that mortality is not the only factor that affects the sex ratio. In particular, differential migration either within or between countries may significantly alter the sex ratio of the marriage market in any particular geographical region.

Once people are married, differential mortality by gender has an impact on the length of both marriage and widowhood. Table 4–10 illustrates that the probability of a couple living long enough to celebrate their fortieth anniversary has increased dramatically throughout this century. (The probabilities assume that both people are married at age twenty-five). In 1900, the chances were slightly less than one in three that a white couple would both live long enough to celebrate their forthieth anniversary, and they were less than half of that for black couples. By 1978, the chances are better than two in three that a white couple will live long enough to celebrate this occasion, and the probabilities for a black couple are closer to one in two. These calculations do not, of course, include the probability that a marriage will end in divorce. Unlenberg's work, however, indicates that couples today are more likely to stay together in their first marriage up to the fortieth anniversary than their counterparts were at the turn of the century. While the divorce rate has risen dramatically, especially since the late 1950s, the mortality rate has declined at an even faster rate. Long marriages are more common now than in the past.[17]

The part of our population that is growing most quickly is the *older old*—those who are seventy-five years of age and older. The increase in the probabilities of surviving to this last stage of the life course can be found in table 4–11. As with the tables throughout this chapter, sex and race differentials are pronounced within each cohort. Women are more

Table 4–10
Race and Sex Differences in the Probability of Surviving to a Fortieth Wedding Anniversary: 1900, 1940, and 1978

Year	Probability of Wife Surviving		Probability of Husband Surviving		Probability of Both Surviving	
	White	B&O	White	B&O	White	B&O
1900	.57	.39	.53	.36	.30	.14
1940	.74	.47	.64	.43	.47	.20
1978	.86	.76	.74	.60	.67	.46

Source: Probabilities are calculated from life value tables in *Vital Statistics of the United States: 1978*, Vol. II, Part A. (Washington, DC: DHSS Pub. No. 83–1101, Government Printing Office, 1982), Table 5–4.

Note: This table assumes that both spouses are married at age twenty-five.

Table 4–11

Race and Sex Differences in the Probability of Reaching Old Age by Yourself and With Your Spouse: 1900, 1940, and 1978

	Probability of Survival to Age Seventy-Five[a]						Probability of Survival to Age Eighty-Five[a]					
	Male		Female		Both		Male		Female		Both	
Year	W	B&O	W	B&O	W	B&O	W	B&O	W	B&O	W	B&O
1900	.29	.17	.33	.20	.10	.03	.07	.04	.09	.06	.006	.002
1940	.37	.24	.48	.29	.18	.07	.10	.08	.16	.12	.02	.01
1978	.48	.36	.69	.56	.33	.20	.18	.15	.37	.29	.07	.04

Source: Probabilities are calculated from life value tables in *Vital Statistics of the United States: 1978*, Vol. II, Part A. (Washington, DC: DHSS Pub. No. 83–1101, Government Printing Office, 1982), Table 5–4.

Note: This table assumes that both spouses marry at age twenty-five.

[a]These probabilities of survival are calculated from age twenty-five, not from birth.

likely to reach both the age of seventy-five and eighty-five, and the sex difference has increased over time. By 1978, women in both race groups are twice as likely as men to reach the age of eighty-five. Race differences persist as well, but there has been a slight decline in those differences over time. The final columns of the table illustrate a radical transformation of the latest stages of the life course. In 1900, it was an extreme rarity for both spouses to survive to age eighty-five in either racial group. The chances were only six in one thousand for a white couple and two in one thousand for a black couple that they would both reach age eighty-five. (These probabilities all use expectation of life at age twenty-five as a base for calculation.) By 1978, while still unusual, such couples are more than ten times as likely. The probabilities in 1978 are seven in one hundred for whites and four in one hundred for blacks.

The Importance of Other Variables. The probabilities presented in this chapter must be considered as illustrative, at best. Several important caveats must be kept in mind as the reader examines the data. Probabilities assume an independence of events that is highly unlikely in the case of mortality in families. Members in a family share the same environment—the same ecological setting, as it were. The shared nutritional status, physical and social environment, access to medical services, safety or un-safety of neighborhood, and social class of family members (not to mention shared genetics) would all suggest that a family member who is at risk for higher mortality shares those higher risks with other family members.

This points to the importance of examining the roles of other variables in predicting variation in the experience of mortality within cohorts.

The national data used in this chapter do not allow such analyses historically, but several variables stand out as being of particular importance. As previously noted, region of residence, as well as residence in a rural versus an urban area, are important factors. It is possible, for example, that race differences may have been greater in the South earlier in this century than they are for current cohorts. The rural versus urban dimension may also have had important implications for specific cohorts. Some cities experienced extremely high mortality during specific epidemics (such as the flu epidemic of 1917), and the impact of these events on families was immediate and long-lasting.

The differential rates of mortality by residence and by race will continue to be important in the future. In the 1980s, HIV infection and AIDS emerged as important factors in differential mortality during early adulthood. Throughout the first decade of the HIV epidemic, AIDS cases have been concentrated in urban areas, with particularly high numbers of cases in New York City, San Francisco, and Los Angeles. There has also been a disproportionately high concentration of cases in the black and Hispanic population.[18] This difference will have a significant impact upon overall variation in mortality by race.

Variables such as region and residence may also be of importance in how they predict additional variables that are linked to the experience of mortality in important ways. Rural families, for example, are more likely both to be poorer than urban families (a predictor of higher mortality) and to have many more children (which increases the probability that one of the children will die during childhood and that the mother may die during childbirth). While this chapter clearly illustrates the importance of looking at intra-cohort variation in terms of variables such as race, sex, and ordinal position of children, a model that includes the true complexity of the social world would illustrate even more extreme differences in how mortality has affected the lives of children in families throughout this century in the United States.

Some Specific Implications of Race Differences in Mortality. It is also likely that some of the factors that continue to differentiate black and white families in the United States can be related, at least in part, to the differences in the experience of mortality. Black women have been much more likely to work outside the home than their white counterparts throughout this century.[19] This difference has been decreasing in recent decades as more and more white women (of all marital statuses) are working outside the home. In the early part of the century, married black women were much more likely to work than their white counterparts, largely because of the low wages and poor labor market available for black men.[20] An additional cause of the larger labor pool of black women is the higher mortality rate, which increased the probability of widowhood in the black population.

The labor of both women and children is one way for the family economy to survive in times of stress.[21] Another possibility is the pooling of resources of several families or subfamilies, including the sharing of residence, as noted earlier in this chapter. Just as Carol Stack (1974) finds that the maintenance of an extended network of kin is functional for modern urban poor black families, such an extended kin group makes sense in a world of high mortality, where death is a common occurrence, and the immediate nuclear family cannot be viewed as a stable unit that will provide security in a harsh world.[22]

We must take care not to overemphasize the importance of mortality differentials in predicting other variations in family patterns, but it is clear that the simple fact that death rates have declined, and that these declines have varied by race, has major implications for how individuals experience family life. Variation in mortality has too long been neglected as an important determinant of how families operate in their day-to-day existence. Death is a central factor in the organization and the patterning of the life course. Only when we begin to provide it with a place in the matrix of variables affecting individuals as they move through the life course can we understand family change and family diversity in the United States.

This chapter has pointed to some of the myriad changes in family life that have resulted from changes in birth and death. Chapter 5 turns to an examination of some of the most important family events between these two endpoints of the life course—marriage, divorce, and remarriage.

Notes

1. For more background information on demographic transition theory and some of the issues surrounding population control, see *The Human Population, Scientific American Book* (San Francisco: W. H. Freeman and Company, 1974); Priscilla Reining and Irene Tinker (eds.), *Population: Dynamics, Ethics and Policy* (Washington, DC: American Association for the Advancement of Science, 1975); and Nicholas J. Demerath, *Birth Control and Foreign Policy: The Alternatives to Family Planning* (New York: Harper and Row, 1976).

2. For a more detailed account of the history of population growth and change, see E. A. Wrigley, *Population and History* (New York: McGraw-Hill, 1969) and David M. Heer, *Society and Population*, 2nd ed. (Englewood Cliffs, NJ: Prentice-Hall, 1975).

3. More complete information on fertility rates can be found in *The Historical Statistics of the United States, Colonial Times to 1970, Bicentennial Edition, Part 2* (Washington, DC: U.S. Bureau of the Census, 1975), p. 49, Series B5-10;

and *The Statistical Abstract of the United States: 1987*, 107th ed., (Washington, DC: U.S. Bureau of the Census, 1986), p. 59, Table 82.

4. For a more detailed discussion of some of the inter-cohort and intra-cohort differences in fertility, see Ronald R. Rindfuss and James A. Sweet, *Postwar Fertility Trends and Differentials in the United States* (New York: Academic Press, 1977).

5. An analysis of the role of boarders and lodgers in the life cycle of families in the nineteenth century can be found in John Modell and Tamara K. Hareven, "Urbanization and the Malleable Household: An Examination of Boarding and Lodging in American Families," *Journal of Marriage and the Family* 35(August 1973):467–79.

6. More complete information on the household characteristics of black and white Americans of different ages can be found in Table 62 of *The Statistical Abstract of the United States: 1987*, 107th ed., (Washington, DC: U.S. Bureau of the Census, 1986), p. 46.

7. An extended discussion of the growth of privacy in families as the result of declines in household size can be found in Barbara Laslett's "The Family as a Public and Private Institution: An Historical Perspective," *Journal of Marriage and the Family* (August 1973):480–492.

8. An earlier version of the concluding section of this chapter was presented in a poster session at the 1985 annual meetings of the National Council on Family Relations, Dallas, Texas, November, 1985. An expansion of this same discussion is forthcoming in a chapter of a volume edited by Harriette McAdoo.

9. See Peter Uhlenberg's 1980 article, "Death and the Family," *Journal of Family History* 5(3):313–320. For an expansion of the discussion presented here on long-term change in mortality, see Edward L. Kain, "Trends in the Demography of Death," in Felix M. Berardo, Hannelore Wass, and Robert Neimeyer (eds.), *Dying: Facing the Facts*, 2nd ed. (New York: Hemisphere Publishing Corp., 1987), pp. 79–96.

10. See Norman B. Ryder, "The Cohort as a Concept in the Study of Social Change," *American Sociological Review* 30 (1965):843–861.

11. National data on mortality vary in their quality from year to year. Many years do not provide data in racial categories. When such data are available, the most common tabulation is in two categories—"white" and "black and other." The 1940 data used in this chapter, for example, do not differentiate blacks from other groups. In every year, however, blacks comprise at least 95 percent of the "black and other" category. While there are appropriate political reasons to avoid the term "non-white," that unfortunate phrase will be employed at times to ease readability.

12. See Alice S. Rossi, "Introduction," in Alice Rossi (ed.), *Gender and the Life Course* (New York: Aldine, 1985), pp. xiii–xvii.

13. See Henry S. Shryock and Jacob S. Siegel and Associates, *The Methods and Materials of Demography* (Washington, DC: U.S. Department of Commerce, Bureau of the Census, 1975); and the *United Nations Demographic Yearbook, 1980* (United Nations, 1980).

14. The cohorts that are compared in the various tables in this chapter do not always correspond, as data are not available for some years on some varia-

bles. The goal is to compare cohorts that are approximately forty years apart.

15. See Sheila Kamerman and A. Kahn, *Family Policy: Government and Families in Fourteen Countries* (New York: Columbia University Press, 1978); S. Kamerman and A. Kahn, *Child Care: Family Benefits and Working Parents* (New York: Columbia University Press, 1981); and Urie Bronfenbrenner, "The Changing Family in a Changing World: America First?" Paper presented at an international symposium sponsored by UNESCO on "Children and Families in a Changing World," Munich, November 22–25, 1982.

16. See Glen H. Elder, Jr., *Children of the Great Depression: Social Change in Life Experience* (Chicago: The University Chicago Press, 1974).

17. See Peter Uhlenberg's article cited in note 9, page 317.

18. See James W. Curran, Harold W. Jaffe, Ann M. Hardy, W. Meade Morgan, Richard M. Selik, and Timothy J. Dondero's article, "Epidemiology of HIV Infection and AIDS in the United States," *Science* 239 (February 1988):610–239.

19. See Edward L. Kain, "The Secret Lives of Spinsters." Unpublished paper, 1982; Andrea Hunter, "Working Wives and Mothers: An Investigation of the Work Decisions of Black Women, 1900 to 1940." Unpublished Masters Thesis, Cornell University, 1984.

20. See Hunter, cited in note 19.

21. See Phyllis Moen, Edward L. Kain, and Glen H. Elder, Jr., "Economic Conditions and Family Life: Contemporary and Historical Perspectives," in Richard R. Nelson and Felicity Skidmore (eds.), *American Families and the Economy: The High Costs of Living* (Washington, DC: National Academy Press, 1983), pp. 213–253.

22. See Carol Stack, *All Our Kin: Strategies for Survival in a Black Community* (New York: Harper and Row, 1975).

5
The Changing Status
of Marital Status

At several points in the last chapter, reference was made to the fact that the meaning of transitions in the life course (such as marriage and divorce) is different today than it was in the past. Changes in fertility and mortality provide a new context for the roles men and women occupy during marriage. It was pointed out, for example, that even though divorce rates have risen in this century, the decline in death rates means that more people have long marriages now than was the case at the turn of the century. This chapter focuses on the patterning of marital status over the last century and explores some of the changes in marriage and non-marriage, divorce and remarriage.

Does the Rise in the Divorce Rate Signal the End of the Family?

The first question in the quiz found in chapter 1 asked about the divorce rate in different years earlier in this century. The popular press is filled with accounts of divorce run rampant in our society. All forms of modern media, from romance novels to popular television shows, reflect the high rate of marital disruption in the United States today.

It is true that the United States has the highest divorce rate of any country in the world.[1] It is also true that the general trend has involved an increase in the divorce rate since the middle of the nineteenth century.[2] By now it is clear, however, that we cannot simply look at one measure, such as the divorce rate, and draw conclusions about the health of the family. In the case of the divorce rate, there are a number of important issues that must be examined.

The first question, of course, is, "What is the historical pattern of the divorce rate?" From 1860 through 1920, the annual divorce rate in the United States rose slowly from less than two divorces per one thousand existing marriages to eight divorces per one thousand marriages. Divorce rates tend to peak after wars, and much of that increase occurred in the years immediately after World War I. In fact, the divorce rate declined again in the 1920s and again in the early 1930s, only to skyrocket to eighteen divorces per one thousand married women aged fifteen and over right after World War II.[3] This postwar peak in the divorce rate was not again reached until the early 1970s. Throughout the 1970s, the rate continued to increase, and it has leveled off and actually declined slightly since 1980.

What exactly does the divorce rate mean? It is important to ask this question when reading information about divorce, since different authors use very different measures of the level of divorce. One of the most commonly used measures is the Crude Divorce Rate (CDR). The CDR is simply the number of divorces per one thousand people in the population. Most countries do not have complete statistics on divorce. Even in the United States, the quality of divorce statistics varies widely from state to state and in different historical periods. The CDR is easy to calculate since all you need is the number of divorces in a year and the number of people in the population. Thus, the United Nations uses this measure to calculate the level of divorce, and the United States comes out at the top (or the bottom!) of the list, with the highest divorce rate.

The CDR, however, has many problems. First, there is no way of knowing which people are getting divorced. Are they old or young? Do they have a large family or are they childless? Have they been married for two months or two decades? Is this the first divorce for the partners, or has each been married ten times previously? It could be that relatively small numbers of people are getting divorced many times, and they inflate the divorce rate each year as their divorces are counted in the calculation of the CDR. (This is not likely a major factor in inflating the CDR, but there is no way of knowing for sure from the statistics.)

Just as the number of divorces is problematic, the makeup of the population also can cause problems in interpreting changes in the CDR. Not every person in the population is married. Many of the thousand people are children well below the age of marriage (and thus divorce). The proportion of a society below the age of fifteen is much larger in countries (and historical periods) with high birth rates, so the CDR would automatically be lower. Similarly, there is variation in the proportion of the adult population that eventually gets married. In a society in which nearly everyone marries, the CDR would calculate the number of divorces for a group of one thousand people, which includes more married adults than the rate for a society in which many people remain single.

In his classic study of divorce, William J. Goode notes that one of the basic causes of divorce is marriage.[4] People cannot get divorced unless they are first married, and the proportion of the population getting married reached its historical peak in the 1950s. It is not surprising that the divorce rate went up in the 1960s, since larger proportions of the population were married than ever before.

These problems of measurement notwithstanding, it is still true that the incidence of divorce has gone up considerably over the past century. The historical patterning of divorce that I reviewed previously does not use the CDR, but rather rates based upon divorces per one thousand marriages or per one thousand married women aged fifteen and older. Indeed, most estimates indicate that approximately one out of every two marriages today will end in divorce.[5]

Thus, we must return to the original question: "Does the rise in the divorce rate signal the end of the family?" The answer to that question is an unequivocal "No."[6] Rates of divorce must be placed within the context of changes in other aspects of family life.

First, both marriage and remarriage remain extremely popular. Most people who divorce get remarried.[7] While the rates of divorce are slightly higher for second marriages, the evidence on marital satisfaction is that most couples feel that their second marriage is happier than their first. In addition, studies of marital satisfaction indicate that most people are satisfied with their marriages.[8]

When we are making a diagnosis of the health of the family, remarriage is very significant. Andrew J. Cherlin indicates that while remarriages have always been common in this country, it was not until this century that the predominance of remarriages are after divorce. He reports that as late as the 1920s, widowhood was more likely to be the state preceding remarriage than was divorce. The decline in mortality outlined in the previous chapter has meant that by this decade nearly nine out of every ten remarriages follows divorce, and not the death of a spouse. This transformation is true not only because of the decline in mortality but also because of the increase in divorce and increase in remarriage after divorce.[9]

Changes in attitudes and laws concerning divorce may also be important in any interpretation of changes in the divorce rate. It is very difficult to know how much of the increase in the divorce rate is a result of divorce replacing permanent separation in marriages. More accepting cultural attitudes, combined with less restrictive laws, may have led to a statistical increase in the divorce rate that exaggerates the increase in the number of marriages that are not successful. A cross-cultural example provides a useful illustration. Divorce is illegal in Ireland (as well as several other countries). As a result, the official rate of divorce in Ireland is zero. That does not mean that there are no marriages that are coming to an end in Ireland. It simply means that marital disruptions are not recorded as divorces.

Many people concerned about the rise in the divorce rate have asked the question: what is the cause of this increase in divorce rates throughout the century? After taking into account the issues surrounding measuring divorce rates, as well as the changes in attitudes and laws mentioned previously, there are several common explanations. The increase in the number of women working outside the home is possibly the most common explanation that is given. (The next chapter focuses on several issues related to women and work.) Other writers point to the women's movement and changes in attitudes about traditional roles. Still another explanation is changes in contraceptive technology, which have released women from the burden and unpredictability of childbearing. Economic problems that face young men are sometimes blamed for the changes in family stability over time. Still others (and I tend to fall into this camp) argue that the 1950s were an unusual time. Age at marriage declined, divorce rates were lower than after World War II, birth rates went up, and marriage rates reached an all-time high in this country. All of these trends were the *opposite* of the long-term historical patterns, and changes since then have simply reflected a return to the long-term patterns associated with the movement of our society into an industrial economy.[10]

Probably each of these reasons holds part of the key to explaining the increase in the divorce rate. It is clear that the many changes that have been affecting family life must be considered as a package. Many of the variables are interrelated, and considering only the divorce rate carries very little meaning.

The most critical point is that transitions in the adult life course that are related to being married—marriage, divorce, and remarriage—mean something very different today than they did in the past. The significance of marital status has been transformed because of the many other changes that have occurred throughout the past century.

Consider the fact that when a young man and woman wed in the Colonial era, they could plan on spending most of the rest of their lives with children in the household. The first child was almost certainly born within the first several years of their married life, and they may have spent at least some of the time in these early years in the household of their parents. High fertility rates ensured that they would likely have eight or more children, with the births spread over more than a decade. High mortality rates meant that at least one of the spouses would probably die before all the children reached adulthood. Thus, marriage meant living in a large household with other family members around. It is likely that the typical man and woman spent only a handful of child-free years together after they were married.

Now imagine the situation of women and men in the birth cohorts of the 1950s or 1960s. Age at marriage has not changed drastically, but birth and death rates have transformed the meaning of married life. More and more couples are delaying their first birth and having their last child shortly thereafter. The completed family size now is closer to two children per family. Since both spouses are likely to survive well into their seventh decade of life, they can plan on spending a great deal of time with the person whom they married. Since non-family members are much less likely to live in the household than was the case in the past, the couple will have much more privacy, much more togetherness, and much more time to learn both the good and the bad points of their marriage partner. "Until death do us part" now means spending *a third of a century or more alone in a household with one other person.*

Marriage means something different for the cohorts of today. Without ever talking about the women's movement, a decline in morals, a decline in commitment, or divorce laws that are not stringent enough, it is clear that changes in birth and death rates as well as modifications in household structure would predict that divorce would increase as family life is transformed in an industrial world. When we add to the equation all of the other changes in family life, including a revolution in the definitions of women's and men's roles, increasing expectations for personal satisfaction within marriage, and the rapid rate of social change in the society at large, it is surprising that the divorce rate is not higher than it is today.

I do not want to be misunderstood; I do not want to be viewed as an advocate of divorce. There is a large volume of research documenting the emotional and financial strains placed on family members when a divorce takes place.[11] What I am suggesting, however, is that divorce means something very different than it did a century ago, just as the significance of marriage has changed over time.

One way to think about the changing meaning of marriage is to look at patterns of non-marriage. We can often learn a lot about a phenomena by looking at its opposite. Thus, the final section of this chapter will focus on changes in singlehood since the turn of the century.

Recent Increases in Singlehood—A Return to the Nineteenth Century?

During the past two decades, there has been an increase both in the number and the proportion of people who are never married in the United States. This trend has often been cited as evidence that the family is in decline. As pointed out in the quiz in chapter 1, however, the long-term trend has actually been a *decline* in the proportion of the population that does not eventually get married. This decline in singlehood continued from the nineteenth century up through the 1950s. Movement in the past two decades has been toward a return to historically higher levels of singlehood.

Before examining the historical trends in singlehood, we must first face the difficult question of definition. At what point do you label a person as never-married? Life-course transitions such as marriage can occur at any point in an individual's life. While people can theoretically marry at any age up to the point of death, most people who eventually marry do so by their mid-thirties. As a result, researchers who study the never-married tend to concentrate on those over the age of thirty-five. A common measure used by demographers is the percentage of a population remaining never-married at ages forty-five to fifty-four. (A further discussion of measurement issues is found in the next chapter, which focuses on how singlehood has been related to the working lives of women in this country.)

Using this measure (the proportion remaining never-married at ages forty-five to fifty-four), there has been a decline in singlehood every decade since 1920. Twelve percent of men and 9.6 percent of women in this age group had yet to marry in 1920. By 1950, the percentages had dropped to 8.5 for men and 7.8 for women. In 1985, only 6.3 percent of men and 4.6 percent of women had not yet had their first marriage by the time they reached this age group.[12]

The overall proportion of the population that is single has also declined over time. At the turn of the century, 20.1 percent of women and 30.2 percent of men aged twenty years and older were never married. By 1970, these percentages had dropped to 10.9 and 15.1 for women and men, respectively. The proportion of the adult population remaining single had been cut in half in only seventy years. Clearly, marriage has become extremely popular in recent decades. Since the early 1970s, however, the percentage of the total adult population remaining single has been on the rise. By 1985, 15.2 percent of women and 21.9 percent of men over the age of 20 remained never-married. When compared with 1970, this increase in singlehood seems dramatic, but when put in the long-term perspective, we can see that singlehood is still much less common than it was at the turn of the century.[13]

The statistics on singlehood can be misleading. At the turn of the century, when a man or woman remained never-married, they were seldom in any type of long-term relationship with a person of the opposite sex. Today, however, large numbers of people live with someone of the opposite sex without getting married. The increase in this pattern has been so dramatic since 1960 that the census bureau has had to create a new category—POSSLQ—which stands for "persons of opposite sex sharing living quarters." This new change will be discussed in more depth in chapter 9, which looks at several recent changes in family life.

Because the transition to marriage can happen at any point in the life course, if we really want to understand trends in singlehood, it makes the most sense to look at the patterning of marital status over the life course rather than focusing on one age category or a summary measure of the percentage of the population that remains never-married.

Table 5–1 shows the percentage of both men and women remaining single during the marriage years since 1890. The data in this table illustrate several consistent patterns. First, in all years and in all three age categories, men are more likely to remain single than women. This is the opposite of the stereotype, which portrays women as likely to become old maids with men being more likely to get married. Second, for all three age categories, the percentage remaining never-married declined throughout the early decades of this century and only began to increase in recent years. Third, in all time periods, the proportion remaining single declines drastically as one moves up in the age categories.

This last point is important. The age of typical marriages has a strong impact on the proportion of an age group that remains single. Since 1950, the average age at marriage in this country has been increasing, so the overall proportion of the adult population that remains never-married has gone up. This does not necessarily mean that the ultimate proportion of the cohort that marries will be smaller, but that prediction makes sense.

Table 5–1
Percentage of Population Never Married: 1890–1985

Year	Age Twenty–Twenty-Four		Age Twenty-Five–Twenty-Nine		Age Thirty–Thirty-Four	
	Men	Women	Men	Women	Men	Women
1890	81%	52%	46%	25%	27%	15%
1900	78	52	46	28	28	17
1910	75	48	43	25	26	16
1920	71	46	39	23	24	15
1930	71	46	37	22	21	13
1940	72	47	36	23	21	15
1950	59	32	24	13	13	9
1960	53	28	21	11	12	7
1970	55	36	19	11	9	6
1980	69	50	33	21	16	10
1985	76	59	39	27	21	14

Sources: Data are calculated from *The Historical Statistics of the United States: Colonial Times to 1970, Bicentennial Edition, Part 1*, Series 160–171. (Washington, DC: Government Printing Office, 1975) 20, 21; and *The Statistical Abstract of the United States: 1987*. (Washington, DC: U.S. Department of Commerce, Bureau of the Census, 1986), 39, Table 46.

Delays in marriage tend to predict an increased proportion of people who remain single throughout their lives.[14]

These data make it clear that marriage is more popular than it was in the past in this country. Despite high rates of divorce, the popularity of both marriage and remarriage provide strong evidence that the family is not in danger of extinction; indeed, remaining single is considerably less common than it was in the nineteenth century.

A final pattern that can be found in the data is the fact that while rates of singlehood have increased rapidly for both men and women since the early 1960s, the rates for men remain considerably below those found at the turn of the century. This is not true for women. By 1985, the rates of singlehood for women in this country were nearly equal to what they were in 1890 and 1900. One explanation of this sex difference may lie in the linkage between singlehood and worklife for women. While the number of married women who work has increased dramatically over the past century, it is still true that, for women, marital status and work status are interrelated. The historical linkages between these two variables are the topic of the next chapter.

Notes

1. International data on divorce rates can be found in a number of places. The most complete data are published by the United Nations in the *United Nations Demographic Yearbook.*

2. One of the best discussions of trends in divorce, marriage, and remarriage is found in Andrew J. Cherlin's *Marriage, Divorce, Remarriage: Social Trends in the United States* (Cambridge, MA: Harvard University Press, 1981).

3. Slightly different measures were used to calculate the divorce rate over time. Up through 1920, the data are calculated as divorces per one thousand existing marriages. Since that time they are calculated per one thousand married women aged fifteen and over. See Paul H. Jacobson, *American Marriage and Divorce* (New York: Rinehart, 1959); Andrew J. Cherlin, cited in note 2; Bert N. Adams, *The Family: A Sociological Interpretation*, 4th ed. (New York: Harcourt Brace Jovanovich, 1986).

4. See William J. Goode, *After Divorce* (Glencoe, IL: The Free Press, 1956), pp. 8 and 9. Actually, Goode's analysis of the increase in divorce is much more sophisticated. He suggests that divorce is one mechanism for dealing with the pressures and problems that are an inevitable part of marriage. He suggests that expectations for marital happiness have changed over time, as has the acceptability of divorce as one cultural solution to marital conflict.

5. See Cherlin, cited in note 2, p. 23.

6. See John Crosby, "A Critique of Divorce Statistics and Their Interpretation," *Family Relations* 29(1980):51–58 for a further discussion of problems with using measures of divorce as an indicator of the health of families in the United States.

7. See Cherlin, cited in note 2.

8. Certainly marital satisfaction is a difficult concept to measure. Most national opinion surveys indicate that three-quarters or more of the married population respond that they are "very happy" in their marriages or "very satisfied" with their married life. This satisfaction varies by factors such as social class, race, gender, and it also changes over the life course. Good summary discussions of some of this variation are found in Steven L. Nock, *Sociology of the Family* (Englewood Cliffs, NJ: Prentice-Hall, 1987); and Adams, cited in note 3.

9. See Andrew J. Cherlin, *Marriage, Divorce, Remarriage: Social Trends in the United States* (Cambridge, MA: Harvard University Press, 1981), pp. 29–31.

10. Two authors who take this final view are Arlene Skolnick in *The Intimate Environment: Exploring Marriage and the Family*, 2nd ed. (Boston: Little, Brown, and Company, 1978) and Charles F. Westoff, "Marriage and Fertility in the Developed Countries," *Scientific American* 239(August 1978):575–580. An excellent discussion of some of these major explanations, as well as their critiques, is found in chapter 2 of Cherlin's book, cited in note 9.

11. For a good review of the literature on the impact of divorce, see Ann Goetting, "Divorce Outcome Research: Issues and Perspectives," *Journal of Family Issues* 2(3), September, 1981.

12. These data are calculated from *The Historical Statistics of the United States, Colonial Times to 1970, Bicentennial Edition, Part I*, (Washington, DC: 1975) Series 160–171, pp. 20 and 21; and the U. S. Bureau of the Census, *The Statistical Abstract of the United States: 1987*, 107th ed. (Washington, DC: 1986) No. 46, p. 39.

13. For an expanded discussion of changes in singlehood in this country, see Edward L. Kain, *The Never-Married in the United States*, unpublished Ph.D. dissertation, Department of Sociology, University of North Carolina, Chapel Hill, North Carolina, and Edward L. Kain, "Surprising Singles," *American Demographics* 6(8):16–19, 39, August 1984.

14. This basic argument is expanded in my dissertation, cited in note 12.

6
Women, Work, and Marital Status

C ontemporary debates about the health of the family usually include discussions of the proper roles for men and women. Both this chapter and the next will focus on gender roles within the family. The preceeding chapter outlined some historical changes in marital status and pointed to the fact that marital status is closely tied to women's work lives. Indeed, many of the key issues in any discussion of changing gender roles involve a careful examination of women and work and of how female labor force participation is related to women's family lives. This chapter focuses on that linkage, and chapter 7 turns to another facet of the debate on gender roles and asks the question, "What are the *proper* roles for men and women in the family?"

Why Focus on Women and Work?

As we look at American families in a rapidly changing world, the transformation in roles occupied by women stands out as a key part of restructuring the way we think about families in society. The image of the so-called traditional family with a husband/breadwinner in the world of work and a wife/housekeeper in the sphere of domesticity seems anachronistic when two-earner households are much more common than one-earner households. Masnick and Bane nicely illustrate this discontinuity of image and reality by contrasting the employment characteristics of households in this country in 1960 and 1975. In 1960, fully 43 percent of U.S. households were married couples with one worker, and 23 percent were two-worker married couples. By 1975, the balance had shifted so that only one-quarter of the households were one-worker, married couples and 30 percent were dual-earner, married couples. Masnick and Bane project that by 1990, only 14 percent of the households in this country will include married couples that have only one worker outside the home.[1]

Standing, as we do, in the midst of several decades of rapid change in female labor force participation, it is easy to interpret the Masnick and Bane projections as indicative of a revolution in family life and the place of women in society. It is essential, however, that we place these recent transitions in historical perspective. When we adopt a longer view, it becomes clear that women's roles have been changing continually throughout the past century and a half in the United States. Careful examination of the data suggests that rather than revolutionary changes, we see instead incremental or evolutionary changes in the roles women occupy in our society.

In this chapter I have chosen to focus on women rather than men. This emphasis can be justified for a number of reasons. The traditional role of men has always included non-household work, so when we are looking at *change* in family roles, it is the transformation of women's work that is crucial to understanding families and the growth of industrial society. The entry of more and more women into the paid labor force clearly has implications for the work and family lives of men, and thus concentrating on the experience of women does not mean an exclusion of issues affecting men.

In particular, this chapter focuses on historical changes in the relationships between women's work and family roles. The linkages of marital and occupational status are systematically examined using aggregate level data. This macro-level analysis is joined with a more micro-analytic approach that looks at the experiences of different cohorts of women as they attempt to mesh the worlds of work and family. The experiences both of specific women and of certain transitional cohorts of women in the late nineteenth and early twentieth centuries are examined.

A complex picture emerges in which it appears that the choice to work outside the home in the mid-nineteenth century was, for women, largely a choice to remain never-married. As one moves to the turn of the century, it becomes clear that work outside the home and marriage are no longer mutually exclusive, but raising children and working outside the home are often viewed as incompatible. Since the 1950s, a new shift is emerging, where larger numbers of women are working outside the home, even during periods of their life course when they have very young children.

This chapter is divided into three sections that roughly mirror these transitions. The first section briefly sketches some of the issues related to the separation of the worlds of work and the family in nineteenth-century America. The next part of the chapter illustrates some of the shifts in the work/family interface for women in the late nineteenth and early twentieth centuries. This section of the chapter also includes an examination of some of the factors that differentiate women's work experience within cohorts. Finally, more recent changes in the structuring of female work and family roles are examined. The divisions between these three sections are arbitrary. Indeed, the changes that have occurred have been incremental rather than radical, evolutionary rather than revolutionary. Our modern eyes tend to discern discontinuous change because we hold an image of the traditional family of the past that defines a woman's place as in the home, separate from the world of work. This traditional family that split the male and female worlds is the result of a truly revolutionary change in our country's history: the transformation from a rural agricultural society to an urban industrial society, which was discussed in chapter 3. This complex transformation began with the Industrial Revolution, which provides the starting point for the first period to be examined in this chapter.

Three basic arguments are woven into the examination of women's work and family lives presented in this chapter. First, while data at an aggregate level limit the analyses that are possible, *it is important that both marital status and work status are viewed as dynamic variables rather than static constructs.* As women move through the life course, they move in and out of the labor force, and these changes are often linked with transitions in marital status. Second, *the nature of the linkages between work status and marital status have varied for different cohorts of women.* The occupational and marital choices available to women, as well as the definition of the appropriateness of those choices, have varied over time. What it means to be married or unmarried, and what jobs are available to women in different marital statuses, have changed for various cohorts. Finally, *within each cohort there are a variety of factors, such as race and ethnicity, nativity, and residence, which help to shape the experience of women in the world of work.*

A World of Separate Spheres

During the early nineteenth century, the separation of occupational and family spheres emerged and solidified as the Industrial Revolution developed in the United States. The transformation has been associated with both the rise of the private family, viewed as a "haven in a heartless world," and the development of the "cult of true womanhood," which made a woman a "hostage of the home." Religion, domesticity, and womanhood were inseparably linked within an ideological structure defining separate sexual spheres.[2]

This separation of the spheres of family and work is the most profound revolution ever to affect the family. The transition from a society based on an agrarian technology to a modern industrial nation caused a split between two aspects of human life that had always been intimately linked. Between 1820 and 1860, there was an unprecedented increase in the cultural stereotypes of women. It is during this period that the ideology of separate spheres solidifies and comes to define a woman's place as in the home.[3] The separation of work and family meant that unmarried women were much more likely to work outside the home than married women. The picture is far from static, however. The cultural definitions of a woman's proper place have been continually shifting during this period of transformation.[4] In addition, the structural opportunities for employment, as well as the individual meanings attributed to work and family roles, have varied by cohort.

Certainly women worked in a variety of jobs outside the home before 1890. The cult of domesticity did not have an absolute grip over the behavior of women in the nineteenth century, and indeed there is ample evidence that a separate women's culture existed that provided a basis for social change in women's roles.[5] In addition, social class clearly affected women's work patterns. Poor women have always had to work.

During the early and mid-nineteenth century, there was a strong link between the unmarried state and specific occupations. Several jobs stand out as being associated with women who are either never-married or formerly married. Indeed, the derivation of the term spinster being applied to unmarried females points to one of the few occupations available to the woman who was unmarried in nineteenth century America—working in the mill towns of New England.

From 1830 to 1860, an increasing number of women found employment outside the home, and in New England, the labor force of the mill towns was predominately female. Thomas Dublin's study of Lowell, Massachusetts indicates that in the 1830's the mill workforce was almost entirely composed of young, white, native-born, single women. Nearly three-quarters of the women lived in company-owned boarding houses, separated from both their families and from men. In 1836, nearly 74 percent of the workers at the Hamilton Manufacturing Company in Lowell were women, and most of them were between the ages of fifteen and thirty.[6] The social and communal life of these single women created a tightly knit community, which led to collective labor protests in the 1830s and 1840s. Rosemary Auchmuty's work on spinsters in Great Britain shows many parallels. They were important in the trade unions and predominated in the female labor force at the turn of the century in England and Wales.[7]

The labor force was transformed in the years from 1836 through 1850 with the wave of immigrants from Ireland. By 1860, 47 percent of the workers at the Lowell mill were Irish. The Irish brought their families into the mills with them, so a family labor system replaced the earlier working system, which had rested on the labor of single women.[8]

While these particular mill workers tended to be young, unmarried women, other occupations have traditionally been associated with women of older ages who never marry. The most familiar of these occupations is the schoolteacher. This association of the spinster with teaching is much more than an idealized image. Educational requirements and social status desires of female schoolteachers, as well as rules requiring resignation upon marriage, had a direct influence on the marital status of women who chose this profession.[9] Richard M. Bernard and Maris A. Vinovskis have explored this relationship by examining records on schoolteachers in antebellum Massachusetts. Women outnumbered men in this occupational category throughout the period. In 1834, 56.3 percent of schoolteachers in the state were women, and this increased to 77.8 percent by 1860. Yet this occupation never involved as much as 2 percent of the women who were ages fifteen to sixty. A static approach hides some important information. When a life-cycle approach is adopted, Bernard and Vinovskis discovered that one out of every five white women in Massachusetts during this period was a schoolteacher at some point in her life![10]

The living conditions of the schoolteacher often forced a choice between career and marriage, thus most of the teachers, both male and female, were single. A traditional part of the teacher's salary consisted of food and lodging in the homes of various pupils—a situation hardly conducive to marriage. The average tenure for the teachers was, however, very short (2.1 years), and only 2.6 percent had a tenure of three years or longer. The researchers conclude that both marriage and other employment opportunities (mostly the former) drew the young women elsewhere. The primary competition for female labor was in manufacturing, which paid more than teaching, and in domestic work, which paid less and limited freedom and privacy.[11]

Although teaching school at this lower level may not have been a permanent career for most women, those who pursued teaching at higher levels (such as at the new women's colleges that were beginning to open) were predominantly never-married females who chose career over home and family. For those in the early cohorts of college-educated women, rates of spinsterhood were extremely high. Roberta Frankfort indicates, for example, that only 47 percent of the 1887–1908 cohorts at Bryn Mawr married, and only 57 percent of those from the same cohorts at Wellesley ever married.[12] An understanding of the complex linkages between education, work, and marital decisions for these women can best be achieved by briefly looking at specific case histories of women during this period.

The importance of the early cohorts of college-educated women can only be appreciated when their position is contrasted with the dominant ideal and ideology of femininity in the middle of the nineteenth century. Barbara Welter's description of the "cult of true womanhood," which existed from 1820–1860, provides a backdrop for the drama that later unfolds when middle-class women begin to leave the home for full-fledged careers and move beyond their short-term work as mill hands and school-teachers.

Women's primary virtues were seen as piety, purity, submissiveness, and domesticity. The advice literature of the day was directed to women as wives and mothers, and "usually the life of single blessedness resulted from the premature death of a fiancee, or was chosen in fidelity to some higher missions."[13] Womanhood, domesticity, and religion were intimately bonded together.

A number of researchers have looked at the lives of college-educated women during this time and noted the strains in their position. Jessie Bernard begins her book on academic women by presenting sketches of the lives of seven prominent academic women who were the "firsts" on many forefronts. Four of these seven women were spinsters, and the other three were married to academic men. The thumbnail biographies presented by Bernard make it clear that the balancing of a career and a marriage for these early academic women was, at best, a precarious and time-consuming operation. To be forging out at a time when the cult of domesticity was still very strong was a serious matter. Of the three women who did marry, one gave up her career upon marriage, and another (Ellen Swallow Richards) started the home economics movement, thus making a career out of the professionalization of domesticity.[14]

Bernard divides the story of academic women into four periods that illustrate how successive cohorts of women faced different pressures in making career and marital decisions. Academic women of today are less likely to be spinsters than were their counterparts in the past, but even today, academic women are much less likely to be married than their male counterparts, or even other women with similar qualifications who are in non-academic positions.[15]

Bernard's description of the history of career academic women in this country has not been without its critics. Frank Stricker argues that the picture is much more complex than Bernard indicates. He suggests that since the turn of the century, college-educated women have married in greater numbers during each successive decade, yet the balance of career and family always remained an extremely difficult endeavor.[16]

In their review of the research (or rather, lack of research) on the history of women in the professions, Joan Jacobs Brumberg and Nancy Tomes concur with the suggestion that any history examining women and work involves "the complex interaction of economic, structural and cultural forces." They further point to the difficulties in combining marriages with a career for women in the nineteenth century, and the resulting high rates of spinsterhood in some professions. They caution, however, that family can act either as an "inhibitor or stimulus to a woman's professional life."[17]

Perhaps the most difficult period for professional women was the late part of the nineteenth century. These early cohorts of college-educated women faced the most tensions in attempting to leave the domestic circle. As a result, they had the highest rates of non-marriage. Frankfort's work on these women explores the lives and influence of two of the "giants" described by Bernard—the college presidents Martha Carey Thomas at Bryn Mawr and Alice Freeman Palmer at Wellesley. The contrasts of how these two women faced the conflict between the ideals of domesticity and the life of an academic woman are instructive.[18]

Martha Carey Thomas believed that ambitious careers and marriage were antithetical, and she remained unmarried throughout her life. Her ideal of the academic world for women included competition between the sexes and separatism in education. As president of Bryn Mawr, she had many battles with the president of Harvard, Charles Eliot, concerning the role of women. She made no concessions to domesticity, and argued that women had equal if not superior abilities in comparison to men. Eliot, on the other hand, stressed that higher education was physically demanding for women and endangered their femininity, their health, and indeed their very lives. While Thomas "loathed images of complacent, submissive wives and mothers," her position softened by 1910, and she began to tell students that an academic career and marriage could indeed be combined. Rather than confrontation, she began to stress social reform as a sphere for both men and women.[19]

The life of Alice Freeman Palmer was in direct contrast to that of Martha Carey Thomas. While she too was the president of a women's college (Wellesley), rather than stressing the conflict between the sexes, Palmer saw higher education as a way of training women to intelligently serve the needs of home and family. Upon her death, the same Harvard president who so acrimoniously debated with Martha Carey Thomas, eulogized the glowing example of the life led by Palmer.

During her tenure as Wellesley's president, Palmer treated the students as one large family. She saw the functions of the sexes as dissimilar but complementary. Social work, in the eyes of Palmer, was not something for both men and women, but rather was especially suited for the moral nature of females. She eventually married a Harvard professor, at which point she gave up her position at the helm of Wellesley to become a wife. She never again had a career, though she was involved in many volunteer social reform movements.[20]

While the cult of domesticity provides a backdrop for understanding the choice between marriage and career in the late nineteenth century, an uncritical attitude concerning the acceptance of this ideology is unwarranted. Patricia A. Palmieri suggests that by the 1890s, economic shifts "had made the culture of domesticity an anachronism." She further argues that the expansion of women's colleges can be traced to a growing sentiment that opposed the ideology that limited women to the world of domesticity. She takes issue with Frankfort's interpretation of the cult of domesticity and points to the need for a more complex conceptualization of the separate women's culture that existed during the period.[21] Indeed, the options available to women were shifting as the United States entered the twentieth century.

Changing Patterns of Women's Work Life

The range of jobs in which women are found expands rapidly beginning in the late nineteenth century, and this period is a time of rapid change in the nature of the female labor force in general.

The female labor force participation rate has increased consistently since 1890, as has the percentage of females as a proportion of the total labor force (see table 6–1). Although the ideology of the late nineteenth century may have demanded that the woman stay in the home while the man was in the world of work, the pattern has consistently moved in a direction of more women in the domain of economic productivity. There have been some fluctuations in the trend, particularly caused by events such as the Great Depression and World War II, but the general trend remains.

As the size of the female labor force has grown, its distribution by marital status has been changing. Throughout the late nineteenth and early twentieth centuries, unmarried women made up most of the female labor force. By 1940, the proportion of the female labor force that was never-married was slightly less than half, and by 1950 over half of the female labor force was made up of married women. Since that time the percentage of married women has continued to increase, while the percentage of single women has declined. The only exception to this trend is the most recent data, which indicate an increase in the percentage of single women in the civilian female labor force in 1980 and 1985. (See table 6–2.)

Despite the increase in the labor force participation of married women, the unmarried woman (whether she is never-married or formerly married) has always been more likely to have a job. The differences between married and unmarried women have decreased since 1890, however. As illustrated in table 6–3, approximately four out of ten single women were in the labor force in 1890, while less than one in twenty of their married counterparts had jobs. By 1940, the proportion of married

Table 6–1
Female Labor Force Participation Rates and Women as Percentage of
Total Labor Force: 1890–1985

Year	Female Labor Force as % of Female Population	Women as % of Total Labor Force
1890	18.9	17.0
1900	20.6	18.1
1910[a]	25.4	NA
1920	23.7	20.4
1930	24.8	21.9
1940	25.8	24.6
1950	29.0	27.8
1960	34.5	32.1
1970	41.6	37.2
1980	51.1	41.9
1985	54.5	44.2

Sources: Data for the decades through 1970 are adapted from *The Statistical History of the United States From Colonial Times to the Present*, Series D 49–62, D 29–41. (New York: Basic Books, 1976), 132–133. Data for 1980 and 1985 are from *The Statistical Abstract of the United States: 1987*, (Washington, DC: U.S. Department of Commerce, Bureau of the Census, 1986), 376, Table 640 and 382, Table 653.

[a]The data for 1910 are not comparable with earlier or later censuses because of differences in the basis of enumeration. In that year, census workers were given special directions concerning the collection of data on working women, and the figure may be inflated as a result.

women in the labor force had more than tripled. The participation rates of the unmarried groups did *not* rise at nearly this pace. These data suggest that during the period from 1890 to 1940, it became more feasible for women to mesh the spheres of work and family. The meaning of both spinsterhood and marriage was altered as a result.

The types of jobs available to women from 1890 to 1940 expanded. Growth in the critical area of the clerical sector of the labor force cannot be understood without examining the role of single women. Segregation of the workplace by sex is evident throughout this period, and it is clear that women in the workforce are limited to a bounded number of jobs defined as women's work. Elyce J. Rotella concludes that the first decade of this century was most important in terms of women moving into the labor force, while the period from 1910–1920 was a time of redistribution within the female occupational structure. At this point Rotella notes a decline in the number of women in manufacturing jobs and domestic service and large increases in the number of women in white collar occupations. The never-married and formerly married dominate the female

Table 6–2
Percentage Distribution of Civilian Female Labor Force by Marital Status: 1890–1985

Year	Single	Married	Widowed or Divorced
1890	68.2	13.9	17.9
1900	66.2	15.4	18.4
1910	60.2	24.7	15.0
1920[a]	77.0	23.0	NA
1930	53.9	28.9	17.2
1940	49.0	35.9	15.0
1950	31.9	52.2	16.0
1960[b]	23.6	60.7	15.7
1970	22.5	62.3	15.0
1980	25.0	59.7	15.3
1985	25.4	58.5	16.1

Sources: Data for the decades through 1970 are from the decennial census and are taken from *The Statistical History of the United States From Colonial Times to the Present*, Series D 49–62. (New York: Basic Books, 1976), 133. Data for 1980 and 1985 are from *The Statistical Abstract of the United States: 1987*. (Washington DC: U.S. Department of Commerce, Bureau of the Census, 1986), 382, Table 653.

[a]For 1920, the figures in the "single" category include the widowed and divorced.

[b]1960 is the first year for which figures include information on Alaska and Hawaii.

labor force as the national data have indicated, but there are clear increases in the percentage of married women in the clerical occupations each decade (12.1 percent are married in 1890, 18.4 percent by 1930).[22]

The case of the entry of women into clerical occupations is instructive. The work of Cindy Aron on female clerks in federal government offices from 1862–1890 illustrates the severe personal and social pressures felt by those women who ventured "beyond the household, classroom, or church." These women attempted to minimize the strain between the two roles by defining their work as a service to their families, yet Aron nicely illustrates the complexities of the personal motivations and satisfactions involved for these early cohorts of female clerical workers.[23]

Rotella's work extended the analysis of women in the clerical profession through later decades. Although she notes overt discrimination against married women by many employers, it is also clear that single women of these later cohorts do not face the same constraints as did those described in Aron's work.

Thus, both the national data on the female labor force and information from studies of specific occupations illustrate that spinsters as well as married women in different cohorts faced different sets of cultural con-

Table 6–3
Female Labor Force as Percentage of Female Population by Marital Status: 1890–1985

Year	Total	Single	Married	Widowed or Divorced
1890	18.9	40.5	4.6	29.9
1900	20.6	43.5	5.6	32.5
1910[a]	25.4	51.1	10.7	34.1
1920[b]	23.7	46.4	9.0	NA
1930	24.8	50.5	11.7	34.4
1940	25.8	45.5	15.6	30.2
1950	29.0	46.3	23.0	32.7
1960	34.5	42.9	31.7	36.1
1970	42.6[c]	53.0	41.4	36.2
1980	51.1	61.2	50.7	41.1
1985	54.5	65.2	54.7	42.8

Sources: Data for this table are from *The Statistical History of the United States From Colonial Times to the Present*, Series D 42–48. (New York: Basic Books, 1976), 133 and *The Statistical Abstract of the United States: 1987*. (Washington, DC: U.S. Department of Commerce, Bureau of the Census, 1986), 382, Table 653.
[a]The data for 1910 are not comparable to other census data.
[b]The single category for 1920 includes the widowed and divorced.
[c]The reader will note that this figure differs from that presented in table 6–1 by one full percentage point. The reason for the difference is that the data in table 6–1 are from census materials, while the information for the last two decades in this table is from the U.S. Bureau of Labor Statistics.

straints and opportunities as they moved into the world of work. These changes have continued since the middle of this century. Before turning to recent shifts in women's work patterns, however, it is important to examine some of the variations *within* cohorts.

The Importance of Differences Within Cohorts

This section of the chapter uses census materials from the crucial period of 1890 through 1930 to examine factors that differentiate the experience of different groups of women within each cohort and also to illustrate some of the changes in the female occupational structure in this country. Race/ethnicity, nativity, and residence are all important factors in the work lives of women throughout this period. Because of changes in the ways in which data were collected and tabulated, it is often impossible to document directional changes in the importance of each factor in the work lives of women.[24] It is possible, however, to illustrate the continued importance of these factors in understanding the work experience of women throughout the period.

Because single women dominated the female labor force throughout this period, they will receive special attention in this section of the chapter. The census data preceding 1890 not only contain a paucity of information concerning the marital status of women workers, they also illustrate the limited number of occupations available to women. The 1870 census contains four major categories of occupations: Agriculture, Professional and Personal Service, Trade and Transportation, Manufactures, and Mechanical and Mining Industries. Over two-thirds of all working women are in only two of the 338 subcategories of occupations—47.2 percent are listed as domestic servants, and another 20.3 percent are agricultural laborers. The addition of nine more categories, which have at least ten thousand women in them nationwide (teachers, nurses, laundresses, dressmakers, seamstresses, cotton mill operatives, woolen mill operatives, farmers and planters, and unspecified laborers), covers over 93 percent of the employed women in the country. Age distributions are limited to three categories: those aged ten to fifteen, sixteen to fifty-nine, and sixty or older, so it is difficult to talk about the life-course patterning of women's work from these data.

The eleventh census of the United States in 1890 provides the first data that are detailed enough to begin to point to variables affecting the labor force participation of single women. There are distinct variations in the employment rates of women by region of the country. Single women have the highest probability of being employed if they are in the North Atlantic states (38.8 percent) and the lowest rates of employment in the South Central states (20.4 percent). Rates for the married and the formerly married, in contrast, are highest in the South Central and South Atlantic states.[25] This variation in employment patterns by region may in part be explained by the differential distribution of racial and ethnic groups in the various states. Race is an important determinant of the probability that a married or a formerly married woman will work, and the nativity of the woman as well as of her parents is an important predictor of whether she will work while she is never-married. (See table 6–4.) Married black women were ten times as likely to work as married white women in 1890, and those in the formerly married categories were two to three times as likely to work. For the never-married, it is nativity that is most important. While only 18.1 percent of the never-married white women of native white parents are employed, the rates for other nativity and racial groups of never-married women range from 30.5 per-

Table 6–4
Percentage of Women[a] Engaged in Gainful Occupations by Race, Nativity, and Conjugal Condition: 1890[b]

	Native White with Native-Born Parents	Native White with Foreign-Born Parents	Foreign-Born White	Colored[c]	Negro[d]
Single and unknown	18.1	30.5	58.4	42.2	42.2
Married	2.2	2.7	3.0	22.5	22.7
Widowed	23.7	30.3	21.3	62.3	62.6
Divorced	42.6	47.9	44.8	79.5	79.7

Source: Data are from *The Eleventh Census of the United States: 1890*, Part II. (Washington, DC: Government Printing Office, 1897), cxxix.
[a]Data for the 1890 census include all women aged ten and older who are gainfully employed.
[b]Terminology from the 1890 census is used here: "engaged in gainful occupations" is usually assumed to mean all paid employment, but the 1900 census reports indicate that the term has "never been formally defined by the Census Office." "Conjugal condition" is the term used in the early census for marital status.
[c]"Persons of negro descent, Chinese, Japanese, and civilized Indians."
[d]"Includes all persons of negro descent." The terms "Colored" and "Negro" are used in the tables drawn from the census materials, but they are not used in the text of the chapter.

cent to 58.4 percent. These differences very likely reflect the impact of social class on work patterns.

The extent to which occupations are dominated by single women varies both by major category and by specific occupation. In 1890, only 43.4 percent of the female labor force in agriculture was never-married, while 87.9 percent of those in professional service, 69.85 percent in domestic and personal service, 82.2 percent of those in trade and transportation, and 79.05 percent of those in manufacturing and mechanical industries were never-married.[26] A closer examination of the marital status distribution of the eighteen principal female occupations in 1890 reveals some very clear patterns.

Single women dominate most of the occupations. Their dominance is most pronounced (80 percent or above) in the occupations that have already been mentioned as being associated with single women: professors and teachers, clerical workers, servants, and textile workers. Occupations that can be done in the home, such as laundress and housekeeper, are much more likely to include married and formerly married women. The clearest example of life-course patterning of occupations for women can be found in the high proportion of female farmers who are in the wid-

Table 6–5
Marital Status Distribution of Women in Principal Female Occupations:
1890

	Single and Unknown	Married	Widowed	Divorced
Agricultural laborers	60.9	27.3	11.3	0.5
Farmers, planters, and overseers	9.05	13.0	76.4	1.55
Professors and teachers	92.0	4.5	3.1	.4
Musicians and teachers of music	79.9	11.9	6.9	1.2
Boarding and lodging housekeepers	13.2	23.2	60.1	3.5
Housekeepers and stewardesses	49.1	15.2	33.4	2.3
Laborers (unspec.)	50.8	26.8	21.4	.9
Laundresses	33.6	31.6	33.2	1.6
Nurses and midwives	50.0	13.1	35.1	1.8
Servants	81.5	8.2	9.6	.7
Bookkeepers, clerks, stenographers, and typewriters	91.8	4.1	3.6	.5
Saleswomen	92.0	4.3	3.3	.4
Boot and shoemakers and repairers	82.8	11.4	4.8	1.0
Cotton, woolen, and other textile mill operatives	84.0	10.3	5.3	.4
Dressmakers	74.5	12.2	11.8	1.4
Milleners, seamstresses	73.4	11.6	13.7	1.3
Tailoresses	79.6	9.6	10.1	.7
Tobacco and cigar factory operatives	76.7	16.5	6.5	.3

Source: Data are from *The Eleventh Census of the United States: 1890*, Part II. (Washington, DC: Government Printing Office, 1897), cxxxi.

owed category. Very few single women in agriculture are in roles of authority—it is only when a husband dies that a woman is entrusted with the management of a farm. Widows also make up a relatively large proportion of women who are housekeepers, laundresses, nurses, and midwives. (See table 6–5.)

By 1900, the number of jobs that employed a significant number of women grew to nearly fifty, and single women made up at least half of the working population in four out of five jobs. The types of jobs in which they dominate remain the same: stenographers and typewriters, bookkeepers and accountants, teachers and professors in colleges, and saleswomen. The only occupations in which widows make up more than half of the employed female population are farmers, hotel keepers, and boarding and lodging housekeepers. There are no occupations for which married women account for half of the working women in 1900.[27] Not only have the number of jobs available to women grown during this period, but the relative distribution of the female labor force has begun to change as well. The number of women in trade and transportation increased by over 120 percent in the decade, with a phenomenal 305 percent increase in the number of stenographers and typewriters, the set of jobs most dominated by never-married women, at 94.9 percent.[28]

A closer examination of three key occupations for women in 1900 will illustrate the continued importance of race/ethnicity, nativity, and residence for the work lives of single women. The three occupations are servants and waitresses, stenographers and typewriters, and teachers and professors. The first of these is important as it remains in 1900 by far the most common occupation for women in the United States, representing almost one-fourth of all employed women. Stenographers and typewriters are of interest because they represent the fastest growing occupation for women at this time. Finally, teachers and professors are by far the largest professional occupational category for women, and the fifth largest occupation category overall.

Residence, nativity, and race/ethnicity are clearly linked in how they affected the opportunities of single women in the occupational world in 1900. This is most obvious in domestic service. In the South, servants and waitresses are mostly non-white. Fully 95 percent of women employed as servants and waitresses in cities with populations of over 50,000 in the southern South Atlantic states are listed as "Negro, Indian, and Mongolian." In contrast, this occupation is dominated by foreign-born white women in the cities of New England (71.7 percent), and divided more evenly between native-born and foreign-born white women in the rest of the country. Race clearly limits the occupational choices of women, as over one in ten of all black women were employed as a servant or waitress in 1900.[29]

White women of foreign-born parents were much more likely to be employed as waitresses and servants than white women of native parents (28.5 percent vs. 18.2 percent). There is considerable variation by ethnic group, however. This is a very common occupation for daughters of Scandinavian parents. Of the women who were employed, 56.4 percent of the Swedes, 47 percent of the Norwegians, and 44 percent of the Danes were servants and waitresses. In contrast, less than 10 percent of working women with Italian-born parents were in domestic service. Virginia Yans-McLaughlin argues that culture acted as an intermediary between the worlds of work and family for Italians. It was not considered appropriate for women to work outside the home in Italian families, and thus their choice of occupations like domestic service was limited.[30] Similarly, Barbara Klaczynska suggests that other groups, such as the Irish, had no cultural norms against women working in the homes of others, so they were more likely to be found in domestic service (30.8 percent of women who worked were waitresses or servants).[31]

Domestic service was an occupation for women throughout the age range, although slightly more than half of the women in these jobs were under the age of thirty-five. The linkage with marital status varies considerably by race and nativity, however. Table 6–6, drawn from a report of the 1900 census, clearly illustrates that for native white women, domestic service was an occupation for the young woman who was not yet married. Black women and foreign-born white women tended to stay in domestic service at later ages. The difference between these two groups is that many of the black women eventually married, but the foreign-born white women did not. One interpretation of the data is that immigrant women stayed in domestic service unless they married, while native-born white women left this type of occupation whether they were spinsters or not.

In direct contrast to domestic service, the occupations of stenographers and typewriters were dominated by white women of native parents in all regions of the country. It is clear that this job was considered appropriate for a different social class of women than was domestic service. The opportunity for this type of occupation was largely limited to women in a small number of states. Nearly one-third of all of the women in these occupations resided in the states of New York and Illinois, and the addition of Pennsylvania, Massachusetts, and Ohio involved over half of all the female stenographers and typewriters in the country at the turn of the century. These jobs were largely held by young, never-married females, with approximately 94 percent being both never-married and under the age of thirty-five.[32]

Even more than the clerical occupations, in 1900 teaching was domi-

Table 6–6
Marital Status and Age of Women Employed as Servants and Waitresses by Race and Nativity: 1900

	Percentage Twenty-Five Years of Age and Older	*Percentage Ever Married*
Native white—both parents native	38.9	19.9
Native white—one or both parents foreign-born	35.3	9.8
Foreign-born white	51.5	12.9
Negro	57.2	46.6

Source: Adapted from *Statistics of Women at Work.* (Washington, DC: U.S. Department of Commerce and Labor, Bureau of the Census, 1907), 50.

nated by white women who had parents who were born in this country. This is true in all regions of the country, with the largest percentage of teachers (71 percent) falling in this category in the New England states. For all white groups, this occupation was slightly more likely if a woman lived in a rural areas as opposed to a city with a population of 50,000 or more. Only in the South did black women make up any significant proportion of the teachers (20.1 percent), but even there they accounted for barely 1 percent of the employed black women. Ethnicity is again an important variable. One in ten employed white women of native-born parents worked as a teacher or professor. Whites of foreign parentage had less than half that rate, but those from British background (English Canada, England, Wales, Scotland) differed little from the women with native parents.[33]

The 1900 data do not distinguish between teachers at different levels. College professors (who would have much higher rates of spinsterhood) and teachers at lower levels are all in one category. It is clear that marriage and teaching did not coincide for white women. In urban areas, nearly 70 percent of teachers were twenty-five years of age or older, and over 10 percent were forty-five and older, yet nationwide, well over 90 percent of teachers were never-married. Race again distinguishes the experience of black women, as almost 30 percent of black female teachers were married.

Data from the next three censuses continue to illustrate the importance of race/ethnicity, nativity, and region for the interrelationships between work and marital status for women in this country. Comparisons between years are difficult, since the 1910 census enumerators had different directions for inclusion of women, and the 1920 data combine the single with the widowed and divorced. Data from the 1930 census will provide the final comparison point for the purposes of this discussion.

The last census year in which more than half of the female labor force consists of never-married women is 1930. There is still considerable variation by region in the types of job that are available and in the marital status distribution of occupations. The never-married make up the largest proportion of the female labor force in New England, where they account for nearly two-thirds of the working women, while in the West South Central states they are only slightly over one-third of the female labor force.

The impacts of race/ethnicity and nativity are also still very strong in 1930, but the nature of the female labor force is changing rapidly. Agricultural occupations, which accounted for one-fifth of all working women in 1870, comprise only 7.7 percent of female jobs in 1930. Domestic and personal service occupations are less than 30 percent of the occupations, while they accounted for over half of the female labor force in 1870. Clerical occupations, which did not even show up as a major occupation for women in the ninth census, account for nearly one out of every five female jobs in 1930. Over half of all native white single working women are found in clerical and professional positions, while approximately one in four foreign-born single women and less than one in ten single black women can be found in these positions. The foreign-born women of all marital statuses are concentrated in manufacturing, domestic, and personal services, while black women are overwhelmingly concentrated in the latter category.[34]

This historical patterning in the types of jobs occupied by women is not specific to the United States. Indeed, I would argue that it is a general pattern that can be observed as nations move from an agricultural to an industrial economy. Women are first concentrated in agricultural jobs and low-level manufacturing positions, particularly in textiles. Domestic work emerges as an early option for women, as does the teaching profession. As clerical occupations increase, the proportion of women employed in agricultural and domestic work declines. Only later in the process of industrialization do many women enter the standard male professions, and it is later still that married women with children start to work outside the home in significant numbers.[35]

In 1930, certain occupations continued to stand out as containing large numbers of spinsters. Indeed, this is the first census in which data allow a detailed analysis of which occupations include a large number of never-married women in older-age categories.

A careful analysis of occupations by age, marital status, race, and nativity clearly indicates that spinsters (here defined as never-married women age forty-five and older) account for significant proportions of the female workforce in public service and professional service occupations (over 10 percent of the female workforce in both categories). The professions are of most importance because they involve a larger number of women. (See table 6–7.) Within the group of professional women, nativity and race both play an important part in the likelihood that a woman will be a spinster. Over one in five foreign-born white women who are in professional occupations in 1930 are never-married women over the age of forty-five. One in ten native-born white women who are professionals are spinsters, and only one in twenty black professionals are spinsters. Occupations which, not surprisingly, include large proportions of spinsters nationwide are teachers, librarians, social and welfare workers, and religious workers. Nearly 30 percent of religious workers are never-married women over the age of forty-five, and another 49 percent are single women of younger ages.[36]

A serious research agenda that concentrates on the experiences of both single and married women in different professions is an essential part of the study of spinsterhood and the study of women and work in the

Table 6–7
Occupational Distribution of Single and Married Women Over the Age
of Forty-Five: 1930

	Total Number of Women in Category	Number and % of Single Women	Number and % of Married Women
All employed women	10,632,227	583,185	646,256
Agriculture	814,766	20,200 (2.5%)	74,011 (9.1%)
Manufacturing and mechanical industries	1,877,989	99,964 (5.3%)	108,662 (5.8%)
Transportation and communication	281,025	5,799 (2.1%)	7,564 (2.7%)
Trade	961,101	49,427 (5.1%)	80,903 (8.4%)
Public service	17,567	1,875 (10.7%)	2,198 (12.5%)
Domestic and personal service	3,166,603	177,675 (5.6%)	284,966 (9.0%)
Professional service	1,525,960	154,671 (10.1%)	58,630 (3.8%)
Native white	1,356,147	131,245 (9.7%)	49,016 (3.6%)
Foreign-born white	103,345	21,830 (21.1%)	5,521 (5.3%)
Negro	63,008	1,379 (2.2%)	3,967 (6.3%)

Source: Figures in this table are calculated from *The Fifteenth Census of the United States: 1930; Population, General Report on Occupations*, Vol. V. (Washington, DC: U.S. Department of Commerce, Bureau of the Census, 1933), 281–314.

United States. The data presented here clearly indicate that, historically, it is in the professions that a significant proportion of white women, in particular, remain never-married throughout their lives.

Up through 1930, at least half of the female labor force was made up of spinsters. Since that time, and particularly since 1950, the linkages between marital status and work status have continued to change rapidly. This is the topic of the final section of this chapter.

Recent Changes In the Structuring of Women's Work and Family Roles

The first three tables in this chapter illustrate the rapid nature of the changes in female labor force participation since 1950. Returning to table

6–1, we can see that the changes of the two decades from 1950 to 1970 match those of the preceding six decades combined. Between 1890 and 1950, the labor force participation of the female population increased by 10.1 percent. The next two decades saw a 12.6 percent increase. This percentage change was almost matched again in the decade from 1970 to 1980. Similarly, the female share of the entire labor force increased by 10.8 percent from 1890 to 1950, and by another 9.4 percent in the next two decades.

The 1950s marked the first time when married women predominated in the female labor force throughout the decade. (See table 6–2.) Further, it is clear that the probability of married women being employed outside the home has increased at a faster rate than the probabilities have for their non-married counterparts. (See table 6–3.)

While the macro-level data presented here suggest that successive cohorts of women entering the marriage and labor markets since around the turn of the century have been able to combine work and marriage in larger and larger numbers, a shift since 1950 is of particular interest. Throughout the past three decades, more and more women are combining work and marriage during the time that they have small children in the home. Indeed, the most dramatic increases in labor force participation for married women have occurred in this group. (See table 6–8.) By 1985, over half of all married women (with their husband present) who have children under the age of six work outside the home. Rates are substantially higher for black women. It becomes clear that we must adopt a dynamic view of women's life-course decisions concerning work and family roles if we are to understand the aggregate trends presented in this chapter.

Table 6–8
Percentage of Married Women (Husband Present) in the Labor Force by Presence and Age of Children: 1950–1985

Group	1950	1960	1970	1980	1985
All women	23.8	30.5	40.8	50.1	54.2
With no children under eighteen	30.3	34.7	42.2	46.0	48.2
With children six–seventeen	28.3	39.0	49.2	61.7	67.8
With children under six	11.9	18.6	30.3	45.1	53.4
With children seventeen and under	12.6	18.9	30.5	NA	NA

Sources: Data for 1950–1970 are from *The Statistical Abstract of the United States: 1980.* (Washington, DC: U.S. Department of Commerce, Bureau of the Census, 1979). Data for 1980–1985 are from *The Statistical Abstract of the United States: 1987.* (Washington, DC: U.S. Department of Commerce, Bureau of the Census, 1986), 383, Table 654.

This change in the work patterns of married women with children has profound implications for work and family life. Issues of childcare and responsibility for the next generation come to the forefront of the discussions of changes in the roles of men and women. These issues will be among the concerns of the next chapter.

Overview

This chapter has tried to provide a broad framework for understanding some of the shifts that have occurred in the relationship between marital status and work status for women in this country over the past one hundred years. The limitations of national data from this period do not allow a careful analysis of the life course of women in different cohorts, but the data do provide a general outline of the changes that have occurred. Throughout much of the nineteenth century, women were faced with a choice between marriage or work in a world that defined separate spheres for men and women. The late nineteenth century through the mid-twentieth century saw increasing numbers of women in the labor force and a gradual lessening of the linkage between work and various unmarried statuses. Finally, since 1950, there has been a rapid increase in the labor force participation of married women, and particularly in the number of married women with small children who combine work and family responsibilities in their lives.

Glen H. Elder, Jr. points to the discovery of complexity in the new historical work in family studies and suggests the utility of an analytic perspective that views family units as "actors in structured situations."[37] Both the aggregate-level data and the more micro-level experiences of women attempting to mesh the worlds of work and family that have been reviewed in this chapter support such an approach. Over time, cohorts of women have faced different options both in the number and in the nature of jobs. Married women moved into the labor force in greater numbers and women made up larger and larger percentages of the total labor force as the twentieth century progressed. Within each cohort, we have seen that race and ethnicity, as well as nativity and residence, have important implications for the occupational choices of women of all marital statuses. With careful consideration for these differences between cohorts and within cohorts of women, serious scholarship on the experiences of women in different occupations at diverse points in time can move us closer toward an understanding of the massive transformations of women's work and family roles in this country since the late nineteenth century.

Notes

1. See George Masnick and Mary Jo Bane, *The Nation's Families: 1960–1990* (Boston: Auburn House Publishing Company, 1980), p. 7.

2. See both Barbara Laslett, "The Family as a Public and Private Institution: An Historical Perspective," *Journal of Marriage and the Family* 22 (1973):480–592; and Christopher Lasch, *Haven in a Heartless World: The Family Besieged* (New York: Basic Books, 1977) for analyses of changes in family life in the nineteenth century. Barbara Welter's "The Cult of True Womanhood: 1820–1860," *American Quarterly* 18 (1966):151–74, outlines the ideology of separate spheres.

3. See Welter, cited in note 2.

4. See, for example, Sheila M. Rothman's *Woman's Proper Place: A History of Changing Ideals and Practices, 1870 to the Present* (New York: Basic Books, 1978), which analyzes the changing definitions of the role of women since 1870.

5. See Carroll Smith-Rosenberg, "The Female World of Love and Ritual: Relations Between Women in Nineteenth Century America," *Signs* 1 (1975):1–29; Nancy F. Cott, *The Bonds of Womanhood: 'Women's Sphere' in New England, 1780–1835* (New Haven: Yale University Press, 1977); and Patricia A. Palmieri, "Paths and Pitfalls: Illuminating Women's Educational History" *Harvard Educational Review* 49(4);534–541, 1979.

6. See Thomas Dublin, "Women, Work, and the Family: Female Operatives in the Lowell Mills, 1830–1860," *Feminist Studies* 3(1/2):30–39, 1975.

7. For a further discussion of single women in the British workforce, see Rosemary Auchmuty, "Spinsters and Trade Unions in Victorian Britain," in Ann Curthoys, Susan Eade, and Peter Spearritt (eds.), *Women at Work* (Canberra: Australian Society for the Study of Labour History, 1975), pp. 109–122.

8. See Dublin, cited in note 6, p. 34.

9. See Harold H. Punke, "Marriage Rate Among Women Teachers," *American Sociological Review* 5(4):505–511, 1940.

10. See Richard M. Bernard and Maris A. Vinovskis, "The Female School Teacher in Ante-Bellum Massachusetts," *Journal of Social History* 10(3):332–345, 1977.

11. See Bernard and Vinovskis, cited in note 10, p. 338.

12. For an expanded discussion of the women at these colleges, see Roberta Frankfort, *Collegiate Women: Domesticity and Career in Turn-of-the-Century America* (New York: New York University Press, 1977).

13. See Welter, cited in note 2, p. 239.

14. A fuller discussion of the lives of these early women is found in Jessie Bernard, *Academic Women* (University Park, PA: The Pennsylvania State University Press, 1964).

15. See Bernard, cited in note 14, p. 206.

16. A critique of Bernard's work is found in Frank Stricker, "Cookbooks and Law Books: The Hidden History of Career Women in Twentieth Century America," *Journal of Social History* 10(1):1–19, 1976.

17. An excellent review of the literature on women in the professions is Joan Jacobs Brumberg and Nancy Tomes' "Women in the Professions: A Research

Agenda for American Historians," *Reviews in American History* (June 1983):275–296.

18. See Roberta Frankfort, *Collegiate Women: Domesticity and Career in Turn-of-the-Century America* (New York: New York University Press, 1977).

19. See Frankfort, cited in note 18, pp. 27–37.

20. See Frankfort, cited in note 18, pp. 41–46.

21. This argument is found in Patricia A. Palmieri, "Paths and Pitfalls: Illuminating Women's Educational History," *Harvard Educational Review* 49(4):534–541, 1979. See, in particular, page 537.

22. See Elyce J. Rotella, *From Home to Office: U.S. Women at Work, 1870–1930* (Ann Arbor, MI: UMI Research Press, 1981). Of particular interest in this context are pages 117–119.

23. The title of Cindy J. Aron's article reflects the ambivalence with which women applied for jobs in the late nineteenth century . . . "To Barter Their Souls for Gold: Female Clerks in Federal Government Offices, 1862–1890," *The Journal of American History* 67(4):835–853, 1981.

24. For a further discussion of changes in enumeration, see Edward L. Kain, "The Secret Lives of Spinsters," a paper presented at the 1981 annual meetings of the Social Science History Association.

25. *Eleventh Census of the United States 1890, Part II* (Washington, DC: Government Printing Office, 1897), p. cxxvi.

26. *Eleventh Census of the United States 1890, Part II*, p. cxxix.

27. Department of Commerce and Labor, *Statistics of Women at Work* (Washington, DC: Government Printing Office, 1907), p. 38.

28. *Statistics of Women at Work*, p. 39.

29. *Statistics of Women at Work*, p. 46.

30. Virginia Yans-McLaughlin, *Family and Community* (Ithaca, NY: Cornell University Press, 1977), p. 53.

31. See Barbara Klaczynska, "Why Women Work: A Comparison of Various Groups—Philadelphia, 1910–1930," *Labor History* (1976):17.

32. See Department of Commerce and Labor, *Statistics of Women at Work* (Washington, DC: Government Printing Office, 1907), pp. 105–106.

33. *Statistics of Women at Work*, pp. 110–116.

34. *Statistics of Women at Work*, pp. 117–120.

35. See Edward L. Kain and Niall Bolger, "Social Change and Women's Work and Family Experience in Ireland and the United States," *Social Science History* 10(2):171–193, 1986, for a discussion of the historical patterning of women's work in two very different Western countries.

36. United States Department of Commerce, Bureau of the Census, *Fifteenth Census of the United States: 1930, Population, Volume V, General Report on Occupations* (Washington, DC: Government Printing Office, 1933), pp. 281–314.

37. See Glen H. Elder, Jr., "History and the Family: The Discovery of Complexity," *Journal of Marriage and the Family* 43(3):489–519, 1981.

7
Men, Women, and Gender Roles

The preceding chapter illustrated some of the changes that have been occurring in the roles of women over the past century. Both the movement of married women into the labor force and, more recently, the rapid increase in the proportion of women working while they have small children have caused many people to be concerned about the future of the family. Because our norms for traditional family roles assign childcare almost exclusively to women, many fear that the shifts in work and family roles outlined in the past chapter threaten the very foundations of our society. If women are not caring for the next generation, the argument goes, then the future is very bleak.

This interpretation of the changes in family roles reflects a fundamental assumption that women are the natural care-givers in a family. It presumes that men and women are fundamentally different from each other and that the traditional role assignments of the past reflect those natural differences between the sexes. Challenges to this traditional division of labor are seen as unnatural and threatening. They are viewed as a danger not only to the family, but to the essential fabric of our culture.

This assumption of the natural differences between men and women needs to be carefully examined. Certainly, a full exploration of the causes and consequences of different patterns of gender roles is beyond the scope of this book. To fully discuss the many issues involved would demand much more space than a single chapter allows.[1] Nonetheless, it is essential to outline some of the basic issues, since they have important implications for how we interpret the trends in family life that are discussed throughout this book.

The discussion in this chapter will focus on several key points involved in three questions: First, "How are men and women different?" Second, "What is the process by which sex differences develop?" Third, "Are gender differences inevitable?" A full discussion of these questions is impossible here. This chapter will attempt only to provide some suggestions concerning ways to think about the answers to these three questions, which are important in discussing family life in this country.

These three questions cannot be neatly separated; indeed, the answers to all three are interwoven. Information from a variety of sources is necessary to provide the tools needed to adequately assess the changing roles of men and women in families in the United States as we move toward the twenty-first century.

How Are Men and Women Different?

The answer provided to this question is much less ambitious than it might at first appear. Quite simply, men and women are different in how their bodies are structured, in how their personalities are organized, and in how their social lives are patterned. They are different biologically, psychologically, and socially. Beyond this sweeping yet simplistic generalization, it becomes much more difficult to make definitive statements about the differences between men and women.

The ways in which men and women differ are not constant over time and place. Evidence presented throughout this book clearly illustrates that it can be misleading to draw conclusions about family life based on current experience alone. The same is true when exploring questions about differences between the sexes. Chronocentrism and ethnocentrism are dangerous mistakes to make in the study of sex differences. Unfortunately, social scientists seem just as prone to these mistakes as is the general public.

One of the most cited sources on behavioral and psychological differences between the sexes is Eleanor E. Maccoby and Carol N. Jacklin's extensive review of the literature.[2] It is usually forgotten, however, that the subjects in the research they review have been primarily middle-class white children in the contemporary United States. While we can find important insights about behavioral differences between the sexes from this body of research, it is unwise to conclude that we understand basic patterns of sex differences in the human population.

Human behavior is learned behavior. It is learned in a cultural and historical context that changes over time and varies between cultures. From the point of birth, babies are taught the norms and values of the culture, community, and family into which they have been born. The rules and behaviors they learn, as well as the ways in which they are taught, vary not only over time and space, but also by social class, race, ethnicity, region, and also by individual family.

Every culture has a sex and gender system that defines what is appropriate for males and females as they move through the life course.[3] The exact content of sex differences, therefore, differs between cultures. It is nonetheless universal that cultures think about men and women differentially and socialize them in divergent ways from birth. It is through this process of socialization, or learning the norms of the culture, that sex is transformed into gender.

Before examining this process in more depth, there are three interrelated ideas that must be kept in mind. First, cultures have a tendency to dichotomize the world into men and women. Second, cultures tend to define the differences between the sexes as natural, and thus immutable. Finally, these two tendencies hide the fact that *on almost any variable you wish to examine, there is usually more variation within each sexual category than the average differences between categories.* Each of these three points deserves more careful attention.

The Danger of Dichotomizing the World

What is the first question you ask when you find out that a baby has been born? Do you ask the weight? the length? the health of the infant? the time of birth? Most likely, your first question is about the sex of the baby. Often, however, you do not even need to ask that question. It has already been answered for you in the first sentence uttered by those bearing the good tidings: "We had a baby girl," or "John and Mary Doe would like to announce the birth of their son, John, Jr." If a couple uses amniocentesis or other methods to determine the sex of their child before birth, they can plan the color of the nursery or the clothes, blankets, and toys that are to be bought in advance.

As that infant grows and develops, the behavior that he or she exhibits is interpreted through the lens of gender. This process continues until the day that person dies. The next section of this chapter discusses this process of shaping baby human beings into adult men and women in more depth. The essential point here is that culture takes a malleable infant and shapes that creature in one of two dichotomous directions—female or male.

Our culture is not alone in dichotomizing the world in this way. Most cultures have a strong bias in the direction of dichotomizing the world in terms of gender. This lens can be so powerful that it blinds people to the similarities between men and women or to the problems caused by a sharp division of the social world based on gender.

Anthropological research indicates, however, that not all cultures think of gender as a dichotomous category. In several North American Indian cultures as well as in some cultures in Asia and the South Pacific, there is a third gender category called *berdache*. This group includes people who adopt behavior patterns usually assigned to the other sex.

These individuals dress, work, interact, and occupy the roles of members of the opposite sex. Often they were given the status of religious leaders in their cultures.[4] Some cultures, such as the Navaho, included a third gender category that was set apart from masculine or feminine; and yet others, such as the Mohave, had four gender groupings, with separate categories for boys who adopted adult female roles and girls who adopted adult male roles.[5]

The Trap of Seeing Gender Differences as Natural

Just as cultures divide the world into gender categories, they also tend to define those divisions as natural. Differences between men and women are seen as the result of natural differences—a direct extension of biological variation between the sexes. While a fuller discussion of the causes of sex differences will be saved until the second section of this chapter, one critical point is in order here. Very few sex differences are universal cross-culturally. If something is a result of a natural difference between the sexes, then it should be found in all times and places. This type of generalized evidence for universal sex differences is difficult to find.

I began this section of the chapter by making the broad statement that men and women differ biologically, psychologically, and socially. Of these three, however, it is only in the biological variation that we can find strong support for universal sex differences.

Biological differences include genetic, hormonal, and morphological variation. Under normal conditions, there are only four biological imperatives that are invariant for males and females in different historical and cultural settings. According to John Money, these are: impregnation (for men); and menstruation, gestation, and lactation (for women).[6] In simpler terms: men, and only men, can impregnate women of the human species, and women alone can menstruate, become pregnant, and breast-feed children.

It is clear, however, that a simple dichotomization is misleading even for these basic biological imperatives. Differences in nutritional status, health history, and biological functioning mean that many men are not capable of impregnating a woman, and many women do not menstruate and are not capable of childbearing or breast-feeding.

Our cultural tendency to dichotomize sex and gender blinds us to the fact that even in the biological realm there are individual cases that do not fit neatly into the categories of male or female. Because of abnormalities in prenatal hormones, some infants are born with ambiguous external genitalia. (The additional gender category found among the Navaho was used for this group of infants). One example of this type of biological error is androgen insensitivity (AI). These genetic males typically have female external genitalia at birth, since their tissues are insensitive to the androgens produced by their testes. Research in this country on AI children indicates that their role performance and personality characteristics tend to conform *not* with their genetic makeup (which is male) but with the way in which they are socialized (which is to be female).[7] This provides strong evidence that environment, rather than genetics, is central in determining the social behavior of humans.

Hormonal variation is not the only biological variable in which a simple dichotomy does not reflect the reality of sexual variation. While most females have two X chromosomes and most males have one X and one Y chromosome, a number of chromosomal abnormalities exist, including Turner's syndrome (XO), Klinefelter's syndrome (XXY), individuals with three X chromosomes, and XYY individuals.[8]

When we move away from biology to psychological and social differences between the sexes, cross-cultural evidence indicates a wide range of human variation. In her classic study of the cultural assignment of sex roles and their personality correlates, Margaret Mead discovered that our definitions of masculine and feminine characteristics are far from universal. Looking at three cultures in New Guinea, Mead found cases in which women were expected to be competitive and aggressive, while men were defined as nurturing and meek. She describes Mundugamor women as poor mothers who intensely dislike childbearing and childcare. Among the Arapesh, *both* men and women had characteristics that we would define as feminine.[9]

Cross-cultural research also indicates wide variation in the assignment of basic social roles. In a study of the division of labor by sex in 185 societies, George Peter Murdock and C. Provost illustrate that very few tasks are assigned exclusively to one sex or the other in all cultures.[10] Indeed, there are only two tasks that are exclusively assigned to men—smelting of ores and hunting large sea animals. None of the activities they examine are exclusively assigned to women in all cultures. To be sure, there are correlations between type of activity and patterns of task assignment. Hunting activities, boatbuilding, stoneworking, and making musical instruments are all activities that are much more likely to be done by men. Bodily mutilation, preparing skins, and planting of crops are activities that are more evenly distributed—in some cultures they are exclusively male, in others they are exclusively female, while in still others they are done by both men and women. Finally, in a majority of cultures some activities, such as gathering wild vegetables, dairy production, laundering, and cooking, are more likely to be assigned to women. The fact that there is considerable variation in task assignment between cultures, however, indicates that biological explanations of gender roles are inadequate.

Neoevolutionary theory points to the importance of the level of technology in predicting social patterns. The relative status of men and women is clearly linked to level of technological development, with women having particularly low status in agricultural societies.[11] Nonetheless, there is still considerable variation within type of society. In hunting and gathering societies, for example, the status of women is linked to the assignment of tasks. C. G. O'Kelly and L. S. Carney have delineated six different patterns of the division of labor by sex in this type of society. These range from cases like Eskimo groups, in which men hunt and women process the catch, to the Mbuti Pygmies of Zaire, in which hunting, childcare, and gathering are shared by both men and women. In the former case the status of women is considerably below men. A much more egalitarian gender status system is found in the latter type of hunting and gathering society.[12]

Cross-cultural research thus makes it clear that biological differences between the sexes are strongly shaped by the cultural heritage of human beings. Psychological and social differences between the sexes follow no universal pattern. Nonetheless, the cultural tendency to see a natural dichotomy between men and women strongly shapes the way we interpret the social world. This first section of the chapter concludes with discussion of a useful concept for analyzing differences between men and women that helps us move away from seeing the world through a dichotomous prism of gender.

The Concept of Individual Differences

The two cultural tendencies noted so far in this chapter—dichotomizing the world into male and female and seeing that division as natural—oversimplify human behavior in a way that misrepresents one of the most important biological realities about human beings: the amazing adaptability of human behavior. The best way to think about this oversimplification is by using the concept of individual differences. The principle of individual differences is the idea that the variation within one group tends to be greater than the average difference between two groups.

In the area of sex differences, one of the simplest examples of this basic principle is adult height. Men are taller than women. We think of that as a biological fact and as a result of natural differences between men and women. The reality is actually much more complex. It is true that, on the average, men are taller than women. But within each sex category there is a distribution of heights ranging from very short to very tall individuals. The difference between the shortest and the tallest man (or woman) in any group is much greater than the average difference between men and women. In most gatherings you will find that if you choose a man who is nearer the short end of the spectrum, there will be a large number of women in the group who are taller than he is. Thus, while it is true that the average height of men is taller than the average height of women, any particular woman may be taller than any number of individual men.

This example deserves further scrutiny. Because we think of height (along with many other variables) in terms of a dichotomized world of men and women, which is defined as natural, we misinterpret the actual variation in height. There are a series of cultural rules that make certain that our myths about men being taller than women are reinforced. Men date and marry women who are shorter than they are (or at least not taller than they are.) Exceptions to this general rule are the subject of comedy. In drama, male movie stars who are short (such as Paul Newman and Robert Redford) are never shown on screen as being shorter than the woman with whom they are portrayed. During adolescence, girls who are early in their growth in height often face particular problems, as do boys who are late. Biology is playing a trick on them and forcing them to deal with the fact that women are taller than men, rather than the opposite.

Throughout the rest of the discussion in this chapter, I would suggest that you keep this concept of individual differences in mind. With the exception of the biological imperatives noted above, it applies to almost any social or psychological variable that is chosen. The variation within one group, male or female, is much greater than the average difference between groups. It is the way that we socialize children, as well as the ways in which we interpret the behavior of men, and women, that convinces us otherwise.

What Is The Process By Which Sex Differences Develop?

In many ways, I have already answered this second question. Sex differences develop as a result of socialization processes that shapes the biological heritage of individual men and women throughout their lives. Because many people might find such a statement controversial, however, I would like to use several studies to illustrate this point.

At the outset, it may be instructive to rephrase the question in a slightly different way: "Are sex differences the result of nature or nurture?" That question has a very simple answer: "No." The differences you observe between men and women in everyday life, the variations by gender measured by social psychologists in the laboratory, and anthropological and sociological records of sex differences in social behavior are not the result of nature *or* nurture. They are the result of nature *and* nurture.

Social science evidence makes it clear that nurture plays a larger role in those differences than most people suspect, but there is no need to suggest that biological differences are absent from the equation. In this chapter, my basic argument will be that if biology alone were the cause of sex differences, there would be many *fewer* differences between men and women than we currently see. It is culture that reinforces differences between men and women so that they are much greater than biology alone would produce in the human animal.

Social psychologists have done an excellent job of documenting the ways in which our culture in the contemporary United States socializes young children into gender roles. Many authors have summarized this literature in a variety of ways (including the three general sources I cited at the outset of this chapter). One of the most succinct summaries of the argument is presented by Sandra Bem. Bem divides the argument into three assertions that are all supported by substantial bodies of research evidence. First, babies are born into a world that has preconceived notions about what it means to be female and male. (In many ways, this is the argument I have suggested in the opening section of this chapter.) Second, because of those preconceived notions, male and female babies are treated differently. (This is what sociologists would call *differential socialization.*) Finally, because of that differential treatment, they grow up to be different—they have different learning histories.[13]

Compressing those statements into one argument, I would suggest that gender differences develop out of a lifelong process of socialization that begins at birth and continues until death. In this section of the chapter, I will talk about several studies that illustrate this process in our country. Literally hundreds of studies have been published on the topic, but I will choose only a few to illustrate my basic point.

Let us begin at birth. While it is clear that the cultural preparation for a boy or a girl begins before birth, a convenient starting point to chart differential socialization in our culture is at birth. Jeffrey Z. Rubin and colleagues studied the parents of thirty newborns.[14] Half of the newborns were boys and half were girls. Data were gathered on all the infants before they were twenty-four hours old. Ratings by the doctors who delivered the babies indicated that there were *no* significant sex differences in variables such as length, weight, respiration and heart rates, or reflexes.

Parents were asked to rate their children on a variety of measures. Fathers who had daughters rated them as more awkward, more delicate, weaker, more beautiful, and more resembling their mothers than did fathers who had sons. Those who had sons described them as being bigger. (Remember, there were *no* significant differences between the babies in actual measurements.) Both parents rated the girls as softer, finer featured, littler, and less attentive! In the first day of life, parents are already seeing sex differences that do not appear in any measures given by doctors. In the minds of their parents, boys will be boys and girls will be girls.

Parents are not the only ones who see sex differences where they do not exist. John and Sandra Condry videotaped a nine-month-old baby playing with a variety of toys. They showed this videotape to a number of college student audiences. During half of the showings the baby was called David. The other half of the time the baby was named Lisa. After the viewings, students rated the behavior of the baby. A single example from this study clearly illustrates the way in which gender shapes the way we see the behavior of others. One scene involved the baby's response to a jack-in-the-box. Like many normal infants, the baby responded by crying for a short while. The student audiences who thought the baby was female labeled this behavior as fear. The audiences who thought the baby was male labeled it as anger.[15]

Young children learn these cultural gender stereotypes at a very young age. Susan S. Haugh and her associates videotaped two infants and then asked three- and five-year-old children to rate the babies they saw in the video. Some of the time, one infant was labeled as a boy and the other a girl, and some of the time the labels were reversed. When questioned, the young children described the female infant as slower, weaker, quieter, softer, littler, and more scared than the male infant. This was true no matter which infant in the videotape was labeled as the girl and which was labeled as the boy.[16]

Children learn the stereotypes not only of personality characteristics, but also of social roles and behaviors. Linda D. Gettys and Arnie Cann asked young children to assign a male or female doll to each of ten occupations. Occupational stereotyping increased significantly with age, but even the youngest group (which was two- and three-year-olds) had developed significant ideas about which gender was appropriate for each type of job. For example, a male doll was linked to "basketball player" 83 percent of the time by two- and three-year-olds, 90 percent of the time by four- and five-year-olds, and 99 percent of the time by six- and seven-year-olds. In contrast, the same three age groups linked "librarian" with a male doll 56, 16, and 3 percent of the time, respectively.[17]

Not only do adults and children define boys and girls differentially, but because of those definitions, they interact differently with infants and children based upon their sex. Caroline Smith and Barbara Lloyd asked mothers who had first-born children of their own to play with another six-month-old infant for ten minutes. Sometimes the infant was dressed as a boy and sometimes as a girl. They found that sex-stereotyped toys were given to the infant based upon how the infant was dressed. When dressed as a boy, the infant was offered hammers; when dressed as a girl, the infant was given dolls. When the mothers thought they were playing with a boy, they were more likely to play roughly and to give more encouragement to the infant.[18]

This differential treatment is also found in studies of parents interacting with their own children, and indeed can be found in almost every setting. Studies indicate that parents reinforce sex-appropriate play behavior in their children even before they reach the age of one, and provide sex-stereotyped toys as early as their first year of life.[19]

Children learn about gender stereotypes not only from the reactions of others and from their toys, but from what they see, hear, and read throughout their environment. The classic study in the area of gender stereotyping in children's literature is an examination by Lenore J. Weitzman and associates of children's picture books. This research found that female characters are significantly underrepresented in the illustrations, central roles, and titles of children's books. The portrayals of both male and female characters in these books were found to be strongly sex-stereotyped. More recent research has suggested that in the decade following the original study, balance in the ratio of portrayals improved, but the types of roles portrayed changed very little.[20]

The effect of differential socialization is that children begin at a very early age to define themselves differently based on their gender. They begin to develop into masculine and feminine human beings, based on the definitions of masculinity and femininity found in their particular culture and historical period. It is not surprising that research on behavioral and psychological differences between boys and girls indicates that sex differences on a variety of measures as diverse as activity level, aggression, fantasy and play behavior, and verbal and mathematical abilities increase with age.[21] As children learn the rules of the culture, they internalize them. The cultural stereotypes of sex differences become reality. Human behavior, which falls along a continuum, is shaped and interpreted through the lens of gender.

A large body of research indicates that these internalized images of gender differences have an impact on self-evaluation and performance. From a young age, girls are found to underestimate their abilities and boys are found to do the opposite. Again, I will illustrate this with a few examples.

Nicholas P. Pollis and Donald C. Doyle asked a class of first-graders to rank five of their peers on class leadership.[22] A week later, the same researchers arranged for all of the children in the class to throw three tennis balls into a box that was concealed behind a curtain. Each child was then asked to estimate his or her performance on this task. Since the box was concealed, the children had no clues to guide them in estimating how well they had done. In addition, they were asked to estimate the performance of all other class members. The actual scores on this task did not differ by sex, although it happened that the only three children who had gotten all three balls into the box were girls. In contrast to actual performance, *both* the boys and girls in the class estimated higher scores for the boys. (The three girls who had perfect scores had self-estimates of 0, 0, and 1!) This finding in the Pollis and Doyle study is interesting in and of itself. Of more interest, however, is the fact that the children's estimates of their ball-throwing ability were strongly correlated with their evaluations in terms of class leadership ability. Thus boys outranked girls in nominations for class leader.

A number of studies have indicated that sex differences in self-evaluation continue throughout life. Rather than review several of these studies, an anecdotal example will illustrate a similar pattern among college freshman. Currently, I teach at a small, private liberal arts school, Southwestern University. Each fall, all of the entering class takes a course that involves small discussion groups and the development of critical thinking and writing skills. Throughout the semester, students write a series of short papers based on readings for the course. For the past two years, I have tried an experiment in my small discussion groups. After I grade the first paper for the course, I ask students to come into my office individually and go over the papers. In class we spend over an hour reviewing the basic criteria for grading, and when each student comes to my office, I go through his or her paper using these criteria. Then I ask each student to give his or her own paper a grade, using the written criteria on structure, content, and style. Using my admittedly small sample of less than forty students, I found an almost perfect correlation between sex and grade estimation. The men significantly *overestimate* their grades, while the women significantly *underestimate* their grades. In fact, in these two years, every man except two overestimated his grade —sometimes by as much as three full grades (estimating an A− when the paper actually had a D−!). Only four women did not underestimate their grades—and in each case they assigned the exact grade. None of the women overestimated her performance, and none of the men underestimated his performance. By the time students have reached college age, the cultural lessons about gender appear to be strongly internalized.

Are Gender Differences Inevitable?

Even this brief overview of several studies on the process of socialization into gender roles makes the power of cultural definitions abundantly clear. While it may be difficult to disentangle the effects of biology and culture, there is no doubt that socialization in and of itself produces profound differences between men and women. One might ask the question of whether or not this means that gender differences are inevitable.

Since the basic focus of this book is on social change, a productive way to think about this question is to place it in the broader context of issues that have already been examined in earlier chapters. The last several chapters have outlined massive shifts in the work and family roles of men and women in the United States over the past century. At the same time, the process of socialization has been shifting. Cultural definitions of the appropriate roles for men and women, while persistent, are shaped by the realities of the everyday lives of individuals and families. As women have moved into more diverse occupations, the role models seen by children in their everyday lives have shifted. As couples have made decisions about their personal work and family lives, they have helped to shape the world and the options seen by the next generation.

As argued throughout the book, I would again suggest that the concept of cohorts can be useful in analyzing this question. Over the last century, each birth cohort of men and women has faced slightly different options in terms of the gender roles available to them. Because rates of change have been faster since 1950 (particularly in terms of women's educational attainment and labor force participation while children are still very young), the options facing newer cohorts have diverged from those of previous cohorts at a more rapid rate. There is a cultural lag between the social realities of the 1990s and the socialization into adult gender roles, which may be at least partially based on an earlier era. Even if socialization patterns change quickly, however, the messages a child receives in early childhood may not match the social reality of his or her early adult life. Cohorts born in the 1950s were socialized with a set of values and expectations that may not have equipped them for the early 1970s—which is when they would have been entering their adult roles. While children of the 1950s may have been raised to believe that there should be major gender differences in work behavior, the economic contingencies of the 1970s combined with the new ideological awareness spawned by the women's movement of the 1960s to create significantly smaller gender differences in work behavior. Even the most progressive parents of today may find it difficult to know how to prepare their daughters or sons for the gender roles of the twenty-first century.

Although change in gender roles over the last century may appear rapid when painted on the canvas of history, an examination of data on gender equality in the workplace or other public arenas often leads one to conclude that very little has changed at all. In the mid-1980s, the median income for women employed full-time year-round was nearly $10,000 less than full-time employed men. In 1985, a woman with a college education still earned less, on the average, than a man with a high school diploma.[23]

While women have moved into the labor force in increasing numbers, as the last chapter illustrated, they have been and continue to be concentrated in jobs that are filled predominantly by women, and these jobs earn less on the average than occupations dominated by men. Just as research in social psychology demonstrates that men and women underestimate the abilities of women and overestimate the abilities of men, so too the economic institution provides differential rewards for adults based on their sex.

A cohort approach might suggest that this will change over time. Current cohorts of graduates from medical, legal, and other professional schools are more balanced in their sex ratio than ever before. As these men and women move through their careers, the nature of the occupational structure will be altered. Nonetheless, the cultural lens that views sex as a natural dichotomy is very powerful, and it is doubtful that time alone will eradicate inequalities based on gender.

The final chapter of this book will return to this question and make some predictions concerning change in gender roles over the next several decades. Before that, however, there is one final set of issues that deserves attention. Closely related to changes in the social definition of gender roles for men and women has been the changing nature of sexual attitudes and behavior in this country. That is the topic of the next chapter.

Notes

1. For the reader interested in more discussion of gender roles, there are a number of excellent books on the topic: Bernice Lott, *Women's Lives: Themes and Variations in Gender Learning* (Monterey, Ca: Brooks/Cole Publishing Company, 1987) is an excellent review of the psychological and social psychological research on how we learn to be masculine and feminine in our culture. Two books that take a more sociological perspective on the same issues are Margaret L. Andersen, *Thinking About Women: Sociological Perspectives on Sex and Gender*, 2nd ed. (New York: Macmillan, 1988) and Claire M. Renzetti and Daniel J. Curran, *Women, Men, and Society: The Sociology of Gender* (Boston: Allyn and Bacon, 1989).

2. This book still provides an excellent source reviewing the research on sex differences. See Eleanor E. Maccoby and Carol N. Jacklin, *The Psychology of Sex Differences*. (Stanford, CA: Stanford University Press, 1974.)

3. The term *sex* is usually used in the literature to refer to the biological distinction between individuals based on chromosomal and morphological differences. *Gender*, in contrast, is used to refer to the social definition of what roles and behaviors are appropriate for each sex as defined in that particular culture. While some authors prefer the use of the term *gender roles* to describe differences between men and women in behavior, I will use both *sex roles* and *gender roles* as

interchangeable terms, since the term *sex role* is more commonly found in the literature.

4. Descriptions of the existence and practice of *berdaches* can be found in Walter L. Williams, *The Spirit and the Flesh* (Boston: Beacon Press, 1986); H. Whitehead's "The Bow and the Burden Strap: A New Look at Institutionalized Homosexuality in Native North America," in S.B. Ortner and H. Whitehead (eds.), *Sexual Meanings* (New York: Cambridge University Press, 1981), pp. 31–79; and C.W. Gailey's "Evolutionary Perspectives on Gender Hierarchy," in Beth Hess and M. Ferree (eds.), *Analyzing Gender* (Newbury Park, CA: Sage, 1987), pp. 32–67.

5. See M. K. Martin and B. Voorhies, *Female of the Species* (New York: Columbia University Press, 1975).

6. A discussion of these biological imperatives is found in John Money's paper, "Nativism Versus Culturalism in Gender-Identity Differentiation," presented at the 1972 meetings of the American Association for the Advancement of Science in Washington, D.C. A good summary of his paper is found in Lott's book, cited in note 1 of this chapter.

7. See Anke A. Ehrhardt and Heino F. L. Meyer-Bahlburg, "Effects of Prenatal Sex Hormones on Gender-Related Behavior," *Science* 211 (1981):1312–1318.

8. A good discussion of the variations can be found in Lott (see note 1), pp. 21 and 22.

9. Margaret Mead's work on this topic was originally published in 1935. The Mentor edition of the book (New York), *Sex and Temperament in Three Primitive Societies*, was published in 1950.

10. George Peter Murdock and C. Provost, "Factors in the Division of Labor by Sex: A Cross-Cultural Analysis," *Ethnology* 12:(1958) 207.

11. Gerhard Lenski and Jean Lenski, *Human Societies: An Introduction to Macrosociology* (New York: McGraw-Hill, 1987).

12. C.G. Kelly and L.S. Carney, *Women and Men in Society: Cross-cultural Perspectives on Gender Stratification,* (Belmont, CA: Wadsworth, 1986.)

13. During my six years teaching at Cornell, Dr. Bem presented a number of lectures on sex roles to my undergraduate courses. I am indebted to her for many of the ideas that are presented in this section of the chapter.

14. This research is described in Jeffrey Z. Rubin, Frank J. Provenzano, and Zella Luria, "The Eye of the Beholder: Parent's Views on Sex of Newborns," *American Journal of Orthopsychiatry* 44, (1974) 512–519.

15. For more of the results of this study, see John Condry and Sandra Condry, "Sex Differences: A study in the Eye of the Beholder," *Child Development* 47 (1976):812–819.

16. Susan S. Haugh, Charles D. Hoffman, and Gloria Cowan, "The Eye of the Very Young Beholder: Sextyping of Infants by Young Children," *Child Development* 51 (1980):598–600.

17. For more data, see Linda D. Gettys and Arnie Cann, "Children's Perceptions of Occupational Sex Stereotypes," *Sex Roles* 7 (1981):301–308.

18. See Caroline Smith and Barbara Lloyd, "Maternal Behavior and Perceived Sex of Infant: Revisited," *Child Development* 49 (1978):1263–1265.

19. A number of studies have been done in the area of toy preference throughout the childhood years. See, for example, Jaipaul L. Roopnarine, "Mothers' and Fathers' Behaviors Toward the Toy Play of Their Infant Sons and Daughters," *Sex Roles* 14 (1986):59–68; Clyde C. Robinson and James T. Morris, "The Gender-Stereotyped Nature of Christmas Toys Received by 36-, 48-, and 60-month-old Children: A Comparison Between Nonrequested and Requested Toys," *Sex Roles* 15 (1986):21–32; and Kelly P. Karpoe and Rachel L. Olney, "The Effects of Boys' or Girls' Toys on Sex-typed Play in Preadolescents," *Sex Roles* 9 (1990):507–518. I would like to thank Shannon Hart for her review of the literature on toy preferences, which I have used as a resource here.

20. See Lenore J. Weitzman, Deborah Eifler, Elizabeth Hokada, and Catherine Ross, "Sex Role Socialization in Picture Books for Preschool Children," *American Journal of Sociology* 77(6):1125–50, 1972; and Richard Kolbe and Joseph C. LaVoie, "Sex Role Stereotyping in Preschool Children's Picture Books," *Social Psychology Quarterly* 44 (1981):369–374.

21. Bernice Lott provides an excellent review of this literature in her chapter entitled "Infancy and Childhood: Behaving 'Like a girl'," in *Women's Lives: Themes and Variations in Gender Learning* (Monterey, CA: Brooks/Cole, 1987), pp. 28–49.

22. See Nicholas P. Pollis and Donald C. Doyle, "Sex Role, Status, and Perceived Competence Among First Graders," *Perceptual and Motor Skills* 34 (1972):236–238.

23. United States Department of Commerce, Bureau of the Census, Current Population Reports, Series P–60, No.154, *Money Income and Poverty Status of Families and Persons in the U.S., 1985.* (Washington, DC: Government Printing Office, August 1986).

8
Misconceptions About Conception

The last two chapters have focused on issues related to the changing roles of men and women in our society. Any discussion of the transformation of gender roles eventually raises a number of issues related to sexuality. For proponents on both sides of the debate over women's rights, abortion is a key topic, with those in support of a woman's right to choose staunchly on one side, and those in support of the right of the unborn fetus on the opposing side. Indeed, in recent years, sexuality in general has often come to center stage in these debates. Premarital, extramarital, and homosexual sex have taken on new significance in a world in which sexually transmitted diseases such as herpes and AIDS have reached epidemic proportions.

This chapter turns to the issues of abortion, premarital and extramarital sex, and homosexual activity. In each case I will review some of the history related to the issue, and then I will present more recent data on public attitudes about the topic.

In the opening chapter of this book, I argued that we often foster myths about family life in past times. There is no subject about which this statement is more true than human sexuality. Four decades ago, Paul F. Lazarsfeld noted that social science is often unfairly criticized for being the study of the obvious. He argued that social science helps to dispel myths about the social world and gives us a more complete understanding of the structure and process of social life.[1]

In this chapter I will present another quiz. These ten questions illustrate some myths about sexuality. While discussing the answers to the quiz, I will briefly talk about the history of sexuality as well as recent changes in those attitudes about sexuality in this country. Next, I will present data that illustrate some of the misconceptions about the history of human sexuality that are held by students (and perhaps by you, the reader, as well). Finally, I will discuss several broader issues in relation to the structuring of sexual attitudes and behavior.

This quiz does not nearly cover all the topics in human sexuality. Rather, it is designed to illustrate a few of the myths we hold about sexuality in past times.

A Brief Quiz on Historical Change in Attitudes Toward Sexual Issues

1. During which of these years were U.S. abortion laws *least* restrictive?
   A) 1800
   B) 1860
   C) 1900
   D) 1960

2. According to estimates by medical professionals at the time, what was the incidence of abortions in 1870?
   A) as high as 1 abortion per 3 live births
   B) as high as 1 abortion per 13 live births
   C) as high as 1 abortion per 53 live births
   D) as high as 1 abortion per 103 live births

3. Which of the following groups was most influential in leading the fight against abortion in the 1800s?
   A) feminists
   B) ministers and priests
   C) politicians
   D) medical doctors

4. T   F: Throughout the decade of the 1960s, women were more likely to disapprove of abortion than men.

5. T   F: Because of continued differences in religious doctrine, Catholics in the 1980s are less tolerant of legalized abortion than members of other religious groups.

6. T   F: University students are much more liberal than the general U.S. population in their attitudes about issues like premarital sex and homosexuality.

7. During the Colonial era, in all thirteen colonies the punishment for homosexuality was:
   A) a heavy fine
   B) dunking in the ducking stool
   C) public flogging
   D) the death penalty

8. The proportion of the U.S. population that currently defines homosexuality as *always* morally wrong is approximately:
   A) 10 percent
   B) 25 percent
   C) 50 percent
   D) 75 percent

9. T   F: Attitudes toward both premarital sex and homosexual relations (as measured by public opinion polls) have become more liberal throughout the last several decades.

10. T   F: Most Americans define extramarital sex as *always* morally wrong.

Dispelling Some of the Misconceptions—Answers to the Quiz

I would like to start by making the same statements as I did after the quiz in chapter 1. Do not be upset if you did not score very well. Most of us have many misconceptions about sexuality, both in the past and the present. Even with the new openness in talking about sex, which has been increased by the recent HIV epidemic, public conversation about sexuality is not something with which most Americans feel comfortable. Thus, many people have limited information about sexuality and subscribe to many myths on the topic. After discussing the answers to the quiz, I will present some data on how a large group of students in a human sexuality course at Cornell University scored on the quiz. That will give you a point of comparison for your score.[2]

Question 1. During which of these years were U.S. abortion laws *least* restrictive?: A) 1800; B) 1860; C) 1900; D) 1960. The correct answer to this question is A. James Mohr begins his book, *Abortion in America*, with the following statement:

> In 1800 no jurisdiction in the United States had enacted any statutes whatsoever on the subject of abortion; most forms of abortion were not illegal and those American women who wished to practice abortion did so. Yet by 1900 virtually every jurisdiction in the United States had laws upon its books that proscribed the practice sharply and declared most abortions to be criminal offenses. (Mohr, 1978: vii)

Mohr's book on the social history of abortion legislation in the United States is an exploration of this transformation of national policy during the nineteenth century.[3] These nineteenth-century laws limiting abortion remained on the books throughout most of the country until the 1973 Supreme Court decision of *Roe v. Wade*.

Question 2. According to estimates by medical professionals at the time, what was the incidence of abortions in 1870?: A) as high as 1 abortion per 3 live births; B) as high as 1 abortion per 13 live births; C) as high as 1 abortion per 53 live births; D) as high as 1 abortion per 103 live births. Most people are surprised that the correct answer to this question is also A. Mohr's research suggests that the abortion rate in the mid-nineteenth century was very high. (This finding is corroborated by R. Sauer.[4]) Indeed, Mohr argues, this is one of the major reasons that laws limiting abortions were enacted across the country. As the number of abortions increased, the practice increasingly came under public scrutiny. By the middle of the nineteenth century, abortion was a highly commercialized medical specialty and was widely advertised in a variety of places.

In addition to a rapid increase in the rate of abortions, the social character of abortion was transformed in the middle decades of the nineteenth century. In 1800, abortions were largely used by young, unmarried women who wished to avoid the censure of society resulting from a premarital pregnancy. Between 1840 and 1880, however, the typical women who were having them changed. More and more, abortion was being used as a means of family limitation by "married, native-born, Protestant women, frequently of middle or upper-class status." (Mohr, 1978: 86)

Question 3. Which of the following groups was most influential in leading the fight against abortions in the 1800s?: A) feminists; B) ministers and priests; C) politicians; D) medical doctors. Mohr points out that the group that was most influential in leading the fight against abortion was medical doctors (answer D). In its effort to professionalize the field, the AMA was at the center of the battle to enact legislation limiting abortions. Abortions provided a lucrative business for midwives, a major competitor of doctors. In the early years of the battle, medical doctors had little success in enlisting the support of the clergy or policy makers.

Question 4. True or False: Throughout the decade of the 1960s, women were more likely to disapprove of abortion than men. While it may seem surprising, this statement is true. Throughout the 1960s, national survey data indicate that rates of disapproval of abortion under various circumstances were higher among women than men.[5] Why would this be the case? With the feminist consciousness of the 1980s, most of us would assume that women would be more likely to approve of legal abortion— which is linked to women's control over their bodies. Judith Blake uses a functionalist model to explain this seemingly unusual pattern. Since the traditional female role is associated with the bearing and rearing of children, it is women who will have the most negative attitudes toward something like abortion, which challenges that role. In data since 1970, however, the consistent sex difference in attitudes has all but disappeared.

Question 5. True or False: Because of continued differences in religious doctrine, Catholics in the 1980s are less tolerant of legalized abortion than members of other religious groups. This statement is false. Traditionally, religious affiliation has consistently been a predictor of differences in attitudes toward abortion. During the 1970s, however, the relationships became more complex. In some years, Catholics who have low amounts of religiosity are actually slightly *more* likely to approve of abortion than Protestants.[6] Among those respondents who have high religiosity, however, Catholics are still less likely to approve of abortion than Protestants.[7] At the end of the quiz, I will return to the issue of abortion and talk more about recent attitudes toward abortion in this country.

Question 6. True or False: University students are much more liberal than the general U.S. population in their attitudes about issues like premarital sex and homosexuality. This statement is true. As with most social attitudes, education and age are both strong predictors of attitudes about sexual issues. Table 8–1 contrasts nationwide attitudes with those held by a sample of students at Cornell University. The university students are much less likely to define both premarital and homosexual sex as always wrong, and they are much more likely to define homosexual sex as not wrong at all. While the data presented here are based on a sample from one university, subsequent data collected from other universities in diverse parts of the country corroborate the fact that student attitudes about sexuality are more liberal than those held by the general population.

Table 8–1
Comparison of Attitudes on Premarital and Homosexual Sex—A University Sample and a National Sample: 1983–1984

	Premarital Sex[a]		Homosexual Sex[b]	
	Univ. (1984)	*U.S. (1983)*	*Univ. (1984)*	*U.S. (1984)*
Always wrong	8.0%	27.3%	20.1%	73.3%
Almost always wrong	4.2%	9.9%	5.2%	5.0%
Wrong only sometimes	49.2%	24.2%	32.5%	7.4%
Not wrong at all	38.7%	38.5%	42.3%	14.3%

Sources: The university sample includes responses on 243 questionnaires filled out by an introductory class in family sociology with 287 students. The national sample is from the 1983 and 1984 General Social Surveys collected by the National Opinion Research Center (NORC). Sample sizes in each year are approximately 1,500. See note 9 in this chapter for more information on samples.

[a]Responses are to the question: "There's been a lot of discussion about the way morals and attitudes about sex are changing in this country. If a man and woman have sex relations before marriage, do you think it is always wrong, almost always wrong, wrong only sometimes, or not wrong at all?"

[b]Responses are to the question: "What about sexual relations between two *adults* of the same sex—do you think it is always wrong, almost always wrong, wrong only sometimes, or not wrong at all?" Responses that did not answer the question or were "don't know" were excluded from the analysis.

Question 7. During the Colonial era, in all thirteen colonies the punishment for homosexuality was: A) a heavy fine; B) dunking in the ducking stool; C) public flogging; D) the death penalty. The punishment for homosexuality during the Colonial era was the death penalty in all thirteen colonies (answer D), although there is no evidence indicating that anyone was put to death under these statutes.[8] While current public attitudes indicate that many people think homosexuality is morally wrong, the legal punishment is considerably less severe.

Question 8. The proportion of the U.S. population that currently defines homosexuality as *always* morally wrong is approximately: A) 10 percent; B) 25 percent; C) 50 percent; D) 75 percent. The data in table 8-1 illustrate that the correct answer to this question is D. Nearly three-quarters of the U.S population defines homosexuality as being morally wrong at all times.[9]

Question 9. True or False: Attitudes toward both premarital sex and homosexual relations (as measured by public opinion polls) have become more liberal throughout the last several decades. This statement is false. Norval D. Glenn and Charles N. Weaver use national survey data to show that while attitudes toward premarital sex continued to become more liberal throughout the 1970s, there was no perceptible shift in public attitudes about homosexual behavior.[10] More recent data from the National Opinion Research Center (NORC) General Social Surveys indicate that these patterns continue into the 1980s (See tables 8–3 and 8–5 later in the chapter). Many people are surprised by this research finding, since homosexuality has certainly become much more evident in the media over the past decade. Central characters in several television shows are gay, a number of major motion pictures with homosexual themes have had huge box office success, and the epidemic of HIV infection and AIDS are responsible for placing homosexuality in the spotlight on the evening news.[11]

While it may be too early to know the impact of AIDS on attitudes about homosexuality, the key to explaining this seeming contradiction lies in the fact that attitudes about homosexuality are multifaceted. Over time, the data indicate little or no change in how people feel about homosexuality as a *moral* issue, but it may be that there have been considerable changes in how the population feels about homosexual behavior and the rights of homosexuals as a *social* issue. Individuals may very well approve of the protection of the civil liberties of homosexuals while not approving of their lifestyle.[12]

Question 10. True or False: Most Americans define extramarital sex as *always* morally wrong. This final statement is true. Glenn and Weaver and recent data from NORC indicate that over 70 percent of the U.S. population defines extramarital sex as always wrong (see table 8–4 later in the chapter). The percentages vary slightly by year, and the proportion disapproving increases slightly if "don't know" responses are excluded from the tabulations. Thus, evidence clearly indicates that people in the United States do *not* feel that extramarital affairs are appropriate.

Measuring the Misconceptions: Some Data from a College Sample

In the spring of 1986, this quiz was administered to a large lecture class (700 students) on human sexuality. The students took the quiz at the beginning of the session, and the questions were subsequently used to guide the lecture for the day. The number of usable quizzes from the class was 470. The students were told that the quiz would illustrate some of their misconceptions about sexual attitudes. An unknown proportion of the class (as many as 200 of the students) had previously taken a course in family sociology that covered some of the material on the quiz. The distribution of answers for this group of students is shown in table 8–2.

More than half of the large class gave incorrect responses to six of the ten questions. The patterning of the responses can be used to point to the types of misconceptions that are most common, at least among students at the university where these data were collected. The questions that received the most incorrect responses were questions 2 and 8. Question 2 asked about the incidence of abortion in the mid-nineteenth century, and question 8 asked about the proportion of the U.S. population that defines homosexuality as *always* being morally wrong. In both cases, the students were likely to considerably underestimate the magnitude of the correct response.

These underestimates reflect two different processes. In the first case, the underestimation of abortion in the nineteenth century is a reflection of an oversimplified conception of sexuality a hundred years ago that equates the Victorian era with a total repression of sexuality. The answers to question 8 are most likely a reflection of the student's perceptions of their peer's attitudes, rather than the attitudes of the nation as a whole.

The students tended to be the most accurate on information in questions 1, 4, 6, and 7. These ranged in topic from early legislation on abortion and homosexuality to current attitudes on sexual issues among their peers. Even in the best situation, however, a third of the class gave incorrect responses. The data indicate that students hold many misconcep-

Table 8–2
Quiz Results of Students in a Course on Human Sexuality: 1986

Question #	Number of Students Giving Each Response				% Incorrect
	A	B	C	D	
1.	208	107	79	75	46
2.	63	181	166	58	87
3.	60	233	59	126	73
		T	F		
4.		245	223		48
5.		361	104		78
6.		313	155		33
	A	B	C	D	
7.	5	21	173	270	42
8.	61	170	140	96	80
		T	F		
9.		354	114		76
10.		229	237		51

Note: The sample size is 470. Totals in each row may not add up to 470 because of blank spaces on quizzes or marks indicating answers that are not applicable. Students answered the quiz using optical scan sheets. Each item included at least one scan of an answer that was not applicable to the question.

tions about attitudes concerning human sexuality both in the past and the present.

Thinking About Sexuality—Some
Important Considerations

These data, as well as your own responses to the quiz questions at the beginning of this chapter, clearly illustrate that we hold a number of misconceptions about conception—myths about human sexuality. The remainder of this chapter will focus on research evidence that can help dispel some of these myths. Two central goals are to provide a more useful foundation for understanding the role of sexuality in family life and to provide the context for examining changes in sexual attitudes and behavior in the United States over the past century.

A useful starting point is to briefly place our sexual behaviors and attitudes into cross-cultural perspective. Every culture has norms that define appropriate behavior in terms of marriage, family, and sexuality. These social definitions of approved and disapproved sexual behavior are among the most strongly held values, beliefs, and attitudes within any cultural complex. Nonetheless, there is considerable variation in sexual behavior and attitudes when the cross-cultural record is examined.

One of the most thorough discussions of cross-cultural patterns of marriage and sexuality is found in George Peter Murdock's *Social Structure.*[13] Using data from 250 different societies, Murdock examined cultural rules concerning premarital, marital, and extramarital sexual behavior. The normative structure of our culture frowns on sexual behavior of any type outside the marital bond. Murdock labels this pattern a "generalized sex taboo," and indicates that it is found in only three societies in the sample. Unmarried and unrelated persons are given complete freedom in sexual matters in sixty-five of the societies. Twenty of the societies give qualified consent to premarital sex, and only fifty-four disapprove of or forbid premarital sex between non-relatives. Many of this latter group allow sexual relations between specified relatives.[14]

When premarital sex is allowed among specified relatives, the most common case involves cross-cousins. (*Cross-cousins* are an individual's mother's brothers' children or father's sisters' children. In contrast, *parallel cousins* are mother's sisters' children or father's brothers' children.) An interesting finding of Murdock's research is that premarital sex among cross-cousins tends to be allowed when cross-cousin marriage is allowed in a culture. When cross-cousin marriage is not allowed, premarital intercourse between cross-cousins is *always* forbidden.

Cross-cultural evidence indicates that regulation of sexual behavior is largely focused on the marital relationship. In all human societies, irrespective of rules concerning premarital and extramarital relationships, husband and wife are allowed to cohabit sexually. Indeed, within the marital bond, cultural norms usually make sexual intercourse obligatory.

Taboos against adultery are much more widespread than taboos concerning premarital sex. Murdock reports that of the 148 societies for which data are available, 120 forbid adultery. It is important to note, however, that many of these societies allow extramarital sexual relations with specified relatives.

Current sexual attitudes and behavior in this country have not sprung from a vacuum. They have a long history rooted in Western tradition. Tracing this cultural legacy is far beyond the scope of this chapter. It is nonetheless instructive to look at the recent past in an attempt to understand our current values and attitudes concerning sexuality.

As with other topics discussed throughout this book, the history of sexual attitudes in the United States is often inappropriately seen in simplistic terms. The extreme repressive nature of mid-nineteenth century values concerning chastity outside of marriage is seen as characteristic of all family life in past time. Historical research indicates that this is far from an accurate picture of sexuality in this country. Edmund S. Morgan's important work on sex among the Puritans points out, for example, that while official church doctrine limited sex to the marriage bed, cases of fornication and adultery were very common in the seventeenth century.[15]

Another illustration of an inaccurate view of the history of sexuality is found in modern commentators who point to increases in premarital pregnancy as a sign of recent decay in family life. Premarital pregnancy is scarcely limited to the late twentieth century. A significant rise in out-of-wedlock births occurred throughout Europe from the middle of the 1700s through the middle of the 1800s.[16] While we often date the beginning of the sexual revolution in the United States as the decade of the 1920s, research by Daniel Scott Smith indicates that the pattern has been more cyclical. Both the 1700s and the early 1900s were periods of increasing rates of premarital sexual behavior. His data suggest that before 1700, only about 10 percent of first births were within nine months of marriage. By the latter half of the eighteenth century, this figure was closer to one in three first births. Throughout the nineteenth century, there was a decline in the proportion of first births occurring within nine months of marriage (down to 15.5 percent in the period from 1841 through 1880). This increased again in the twentieth century.[17]

Why did premarital sexual activity decline during the nineteenth century? Any explanation cannot ignore the broader societal shifts that have been discussed in earlier chapters. Changes in gender roles associated with the growth of industrial capitalism and increased urbanization helped develop new attitudes about sexuality. Just as the "cult of true womanhood" reshaped the definitions of male and female roles, a nineteenth-century ideology developed that viewed men and women as very different in their sexuality. Men were viewed as sexual beings, while women were the source of religious and moral strength. The epitome of this dichotomous view of sexuality is illustrated by the large number of late nineteenth-century women who, rather than experiencing sexual pleasure, chose to have gynecological surgery, including clitoridectomies.[18]

This nineteenth-century world of sexuality was based on what one historian has called a "spermatic economy"—the notion that there is a limited amount of sexual energy in the body. When an individual has expended this resource, energy from other organs in the body will be drawn upon. This explains the prohibitions on masturbation or excessive sexual license common throughout the nineteenth century. Once the sexual energy had been used, energy from the brain would be drained away, leading to sunken eyes, sallow complexion, and even insanity. This model of sexuality was even used to condemn women who pursued a higher education. Since a correlation was found between low fertility and college education of women, it was suggested that a woman's use of too much intellectual energy sapped away power from her reproductive system!

While these nineteenth-century views may seem quaint from our vantage point, they provide the foundation for current attitudes and values about sexuality. The firmly entrenched double standard of sexual morality is rooted in this cultural tradition.

Recent Changes in Sexual Attitudes and Behavior

Accurately measuring changes in sexual behavior and attitudes is a difficult task. It is impossible to directly observe a set of behaviors that are defined by the culture as private activity. Indeed, there are no good data on sexual behavior in this country that are based on representative national samples of the population.[19] A number of studies, however, have measured premarital sexual activity in the United States using samples of a more limited scope. Evidence indicates that the majority of both men and women have had sexual intercourse before the age of eighteen, with slightly higher rates being found among men.[20]

Trends in sexual behavior during the last several decades can be summarized by looking at the findings of two major studies of sexual behavior—the Kinsey studies, which report on data collected between 1938 and 1949, and research by Morton Hunt, based on data gathered in 1972.[21] A comparison of these two sets of data indicates an increase in premarital sexual activity over time, with the largest change found among women. The result is that the sex difference in premarital sexual experience has declined over time. (This is offset by a decline in men's early experience with prostitutes.)

These same two sets of data indicate an increase in the frequency of coitus among married couples in all age groups. There is also an increased acceptance of oral sex in both premarital and marital sexual interactions, and an increased acceptance of anal intercourse in married couples.

Finally, a comparison of the Kinsey and Hunt research does *not* suggest any significant increases in extramarital sexual behavior, with the exception of the rates found among younger women. In both samples, men had higher rates (ranging from 30 percent to 47 percent indicating they had ever had extramarital intercourse) than women (whose rates ranged from 8 percent to 24 percent). A more recent study by Philip Blumstein and Pepper Schwartz found that rates of extramarital sexual activity increased significantly with the length of the marriage, and that the difference in rates between men and women in heterosexual couples has declined.[22]

The quality of data and number of studies on attitudes about sexuality are significantly better than those on behavior. As with the information

Table 8–3
Attitudes Toward Premarital Sex: Selected Years, 1972–1988

Year	AW	AAW	WOS	NWAA
1972	36.6%	11.8%	24.3%	27.3%
1974	33	12.7	23.6	30.7
1975	30.9	12.3	24	32.8
1977	31	9.5	23	36.5
1978	29.3	11.7	20.3	38.7
1982	28.6	9.1	21.3	41
1988	26.3	10.7	22.4	40.6

Source: Data are drawn from the NORC General Social Surveys (see note 24 in this chapter).

Note: Responses are to the question, "There's been a lot of discussion about the way morals and attitudes about sex are changing in this country. If a man and a woman have sex relations before marriage, do you think it is always wrong, almost always wrong, wrong only sometimes, or not wrong at all?" In this table, the acronyms AW, AAW, WOS, and NWAA are used to refer to these answers. Respondents who did not answer the question or who responded that they did not know were excluded from the analysis.

on behavior, it appears that since the 1940s, there has been a decline in the double standard, with fewer people defining premarital sexual behavior as appropriate for men but not for women.[23] Indeed, one of the most striking changes in sexual attitudes over the past several decades has been a continuing decline in the proportion of the U.S. population who define premarital sex as wrong. This trend has been occurring at least since the beginning of the 1960s and is reflected in data from the last two decades as reported in table 8–3. Between 1972 and 1988, the proportion of the U.S. population indicating that premarital sex was always wrong declined from more than one-third to scarcely one-quarter. On the opposite end of the scale, the proportion holding the opinion that premarital sex is not wrong at all increased from slightly above one-quarter of the population to more than four out of every ten people.[24]

It is important to note that this question is clearly measuring respondent's attitudes toward premarital sex between *adults*. In 1988, the NORC General Social Survey also asked a question about premarital sex between teenagers. The question read, "What if they are in their early teens, say 14 to 16 years old? In that case, do you think sex relations before marriage are always wrong, almost always wrong, wrong only sometimes, or not wrong at all?" In the same sample, 69.4 percent of respondents indicated that this behavior was always wrong, and another 16.2 percent indicated it was almost always wrong. Only 11.1 percent felt premarital sex among teenagers was wrong only sometimes, and a scant 3.3 percent indicated it was not wrong at all. This variation in responses indicates that the wording of questions is very important, and attitudes often have multiple dimensions—two points to which we will return later in this chapter.

In the quiz at the beginning of this chapter, it was pointed out that patterns in attitudes toward extramarital sex and homosexual behavior have not followed a similar trend toward more permissiveness. Tables 8–4 and 8–5 illustrate this, using two more questions drawn from the General Social Surveys. In general, between 1972 and 1988, there has been no directional trend in attitudes toward extramarital and homosexual behavior. In both cases, a large majority of the population define the behavior as wrong at all times. There is one exception to this generalization, however. The data for 1984 and 1988 on extramarital sex indicate a slight decline in the proportion of the population indicating that extramarital sex is either wrong only sometimes or not wrong at all and an increase in the proportion of the population defining this behavior as always wrong. By 1988, less than 8 percent of the respondents felt that it was wrong only sometimes or not wrong at all. The most obvious explanation of this shift is a response to the HIV epidemic. It is interesting to note that a directional trend of this strength is not reflected in the data on attitudes concerning homosexual behavior (see table 8–5). The measure on premarital sex also provides no evidence that attitudes have shifted in a more restrictive direction during the 1980s as a result of concern about AIDS.

Recent Trends in Attitudes Toward Abortion

An issue of continuing political concern in the last decades of the twentieth century is the legal status of abortion. The first questions in the quiz that opened this chapter pointed to the sweeping changes in abortion attitudes, practices, and laws in the United States during the nineteenth century. By the end of the nineteenth century, abortion was illegal in all states in the country. Attitudes shifted throughout this century, however, and by the beginning of the 1960s, a majority of the population favored legal abortion in the so-called hard cases, in which the mother's health was in danger, there was a chance of a serious birth defect in the child, or the pregnancy was a result of rape. More than half of the population disapproved of abortion, however, for the so-called soft cases, in which abortion was desired because of economic hardship or as a method to limit family size.[25]

Throughout the last three decades, there have been two clear dimensions in abortion attitudes. A majority of the population has consistently supported legal abortion for the hard cases. Smaller proportions of the population support legal abortion in the soft cases. During the same time period, there has been more variation in attitudes on the soft reasons for

Table 8–4
Attitudes Toward Extramarital Sex: Selected Years, 1973–1988

Year	AW	AAW	WOS	NWAA
1973	69.6%	14.7%	11.6%	4.1%
1974	74.1	11.8	11.6	2.5
1976	68.7	15.6	11.5	4.3
1977	73	13.6	10.1	3.2
1980	70.5	15.9	9.9	3.7
1982	73.4	13.4	10.4	2.8
1984	70.6	18.2	8.9	2.3
1988	79.3	13	5.6	2.1

Source: Data are drawn from the NORC General Social Surveys (see note 24 in this chapter).

Note: Responses are to the question: "What is your opinion about a *married* person having sexual relations with someone *other* than the marriage partner—is it always wrong, almost always wrong, wrong only sometimes, or not wrong at all?" In this table, the acronyms AW, AAW, WOS, and NWAA are used to refer to these answers. Respondents who did not answer the question or who responded that they did not know were excluded from the analysis.

abortion (poverty, family limitation, premarital pregnancy) than on the hard reasons (mother's health, defect in the child, rape). Changes in abortion attitudes since the early 1970s have followed an interesting pattern. While there have been small fluctuations in attitudes, the most striking changes have been found after Supreme Court decisions. As data in table

Table 8–5
Attitudes Toward Homosexual Sex: Selected Years, 1973–1988

Year	AW	AAW	WOS	NWAA
1973	74.3%	6.7%	7.8%	11.2%
1974	73.1	5.2	8.2	13.5
1976	70.1	6.2	7.8	15.9
1977	71.8	5.8	7.5	14.9
1980	73.3	6.1	6	14.6
1982	73.4	5.3	6.6	14.7
1984	73.3	5	7.4	14.3
1988	76.8	4.7	5.7	12.8

Source: Data are drawn from the NORC General Social Surveys (see note 24 in this chapter).

Note: Responses are to the question: "What about sexual relations between two *adults* of the same sex—do you think it is always wrong, almost always wrong, wrong only sometimes, or not wrong at all?" In this table, the acronyms AW, AAW, WOS, and NWAA are used to refer to these answers. Respondents who did not answer the question or who responded that they did not know were excluded from the analysis.

Table 8–6
Changes in Abortion Attitudes: Selected Years, 1972–1988

						Percentage Change in Those Approving by Year						
Reason	1972[a]	1973	1974	1975	1976	1977	1978	1980	1982	1983	1984	1988
Defect	78.6	+5.9	+ .6	−1.9	+ .7	+1.6	−3.5	+1.1	+1.3	−5.5	+1.3	− 1.4 (78.8)
Health	86.9	+5.4	+ .1	−1.7	+ .1	− .3	+ .1	− .5	+1.7	−2.1	− .2	− .8(88.7)
Rape	79.1	+4.4	+3.0	−2.8	—	+ .1	− .6	+ .2	+3.5	−4.1	−2.4	+ .7(81.1)
No more	39.7	+8.0	− .8	−1.2	+ .5	+ .3	−6.2	+6.8	+1.4	−9.6	+3.8	− 2.8(39.9)
Poor	48.8	+4.6	+1.4	−1.6	− .1	+ .3	−6.0	+4.3	+ .2	−8.2	+2.5	− 4.2 (42)
Single	43.5	+4.4	+3.0	−2.8	—	+ .1	− .6	+ .2	+3.5	−4.1	+4.8	−12.6 (39.4)

Source: Data are drawn from the NORC General Social Surveys (see note 24 in this chapter).
Note: Responses are to the question: "Please tell me whether or not *you* think it should be possible for a pregnant woman to obtain a *legal* abortion if . . . there is a strong chance of serious defect in the baby; she is married and does not want any more children; the woman's own health is seriously endangered by the pregnancy; the family has a very low income and cannot afford any more children; she became pregnant as a result of rape; she is not married and does not want to marry the man." Respondents who did not answer the question and those who indicated that they did not know are excluded from the analysis.
[a]1972 is the base year in this table. This column indicates the percentage approving of legal abortion under the circumstance listed. Other columns indicate the percentage change between the two years of measurement.

8–6 illustrate, attitudes on all six measures became more permissive of legal abortion after the *Roe v. Wade* decision in 1973. Attitudes on all six measures became more restrictive after the Supreme Court decision limiting Medicaid funding for abortions a decade later. The most striking change in recent years is a decline in support for legal abortion in the soft cases, particularly if the woman is single and does not want to marry the man. This is interesting, given the concern over the rising rate of teenage premarital pregnancy.

This brief look at recent trends in abortion attitudes makes it clear that the patterning of attitudes on sexual issues is very complex and subject to change over time. Predicting future patterning of sexual attitudes and behavior is difficult because of the influence of political and legal decisions on public attitudes. The final chapter turns to predictions for the future and outlines a series of guidelines for thinking about future changes in family life in the United States.

Notes

1. See Paul F. Lazarsfeld, "What is Obvious?" *Public Opinion Quarterly* 13(1949):378–380.

2. I would like to thank Dr. Andrea Parrot for allowing me to collect the data that are presented in this chapter. They were collected in her human sexuality class at Cornell University. I would also like to thank Mr. Jay Coburn for his assistance in data analysis for the section of this chapter on student attitudes in Dr. Parrot's class at Cornell.

3. This excellent book by Mohr is the source of the historical information on abortion used in this chapter. For further information, see James C. Mohr, *Abortion in America: The Origins and Evolution of National Policy* (New York: Oxford University Press, 1978).

4. See R. Sauer, "Attitudes to Abortion in America, 1800–1973," *Population Studies* 28(1974):53–67.

5. A review of abortion attitudes in the 1960s is found in Judith Blake's article, "Abortion and Public Opinion: The 1960–1970 Decade," *Science* 171 (1971):540–549.

6. See W.R. Arney and W.H. Trescher, "Trends in Attitudes Toward Abortion, 1972–1975," *Family Planning Perspectives* 8(3):117–124, 1976.

7. For more on the analysis of abortion attitudes during the decade of the 1970s, see the article cited in note 6 as well as L. M. Tedrow and E. R. Mahoney, "Trends in Attitudes Toward Abortion: 1972–1976," *Public Opinion Quarterly* 38(2):159–173.

8. See Louis Crompton, "Homosexuals and the Death Penalty in Colonial America," *Journal of Homosexuality* 1(3):277–293.

9. James Allan Davis, Principal Investigator, and Tom W. Smith, Senior Study Director, *General Social Surveys, 1972–1983: Cumulative Codebook.* (Chicago: National Opinion Research Center, 1983).

10. See Norval D.Glenn and Charles N. Weaver, "Attitudes Toward Premarital, Extramarital, and Homosexual Relations in the U.S. in the 1970s," *The Journal of Sex Research* 15(1979):108–118.

11. It is important to note that AIDS is *not* a disease of homosexuals. The early conceptualizations of the disease in this country linked AIDS and HIV infection with groups that are typically defined as deviant—homosexual men and intravenous drug users. This social definition has been important in public response to the epidemic. For a further discussion of this issue, see Edward Albert, "Illness and Deviance: The Response of the Press to AIDS," in Douglas A. Feldman and Thomas M. Johnson (eds), *The Social Dimensions of AIDS: Methods and Theory* (New York: Praeger, 1986), pp. 163–178; Dennis Altman, *AIDS in the Mind of America* (Garden City: Anchor Press/Doubleday, 1986); Allan M. Brandt, *No Magic Bullet* (New York: Oxford University Press, 1986); and Edward L. Kain, "A Note on the Integration of AIDS into the Sociology of Human Sexuality," *Teaching Sociology*, 15(1987):320–323.

12. Data from the National Opinion Research Center's General Social Surveys do indeed indicate that there has been an increase in the support for civil liberties of homosexuals over time. See my chapter, "The Federal Government Should Not Foster Legislation Relating to the Family," in Harold Feldman and Andrea Parrot (eds.), *Human Sexuality: Contemporary Controversies* (Beverly Hills: Sage, 1984), pp. 276–292.

13. George Peter Murdock, *Social Structure* (New York: Free Press, 1965). For further information on variation in sexual practices, with a particular focus on homosexuality, see Vern L. Bullough, *Sexual Variance in Society and History* (Chicago: University of Chicago Press, 1976).

14. See Murdock (cited in note 13), chapters 1 and 9.

15. See Edmund S. Morgan, "The Puritans and Sex," *New England Quarterly* (December 1942:591–607).

16. For a further discussion of this historical shift, see Edward Shorter's "Illegitimacy, Sexual Revolution, and Social Change in Modern Europe," *Journal of Interdisciplinary History* 2(Autumm 1971):237–272.

17. For a more complete discussion of these shifts, see Daniel Scott Smith, "The Dating of the American Sexual Revolution: Evidence and Interpretation," in Michael Gordon (ed.), *The American Family in Social-Historical Perspective* (New York: St. Martin's Press, 1973), pp. 321–335.

18. A fascinating discussion of nineteenth-century sexuality is found in Ben Barker-Benfield's "The Spermatic Economy: A Nineteenth-Century View of Sexuality," *Feminist Studies* 1(1), 1972.

19. For a review of recent studies of sexual behavior, see June Machover Reinisch, Stephanie A. Sanders, and Mary Ziemba-Davis, "The Study of Sexual Behavior in Relation to the Transmission of Human Immunodeficiency Virus," *American Psychologist* 43(11):921–927, 1988.

20. A good source of data on premarital sexuality is found in DeLameter and MacCorquodale, *Premarital Sexuality: Attitudes, Relationships, Behavior* (Madison: University of Wisconsin Press, 1979). See also I. L. Reiss, *The Social Context of Premarital Sexual Permissiveness* (New York: Holt, Rinehart & Winston, 1967).

21. For more information on these sets of data, see A.C. Kinsey, W. Pomeroy, and C. Martin, *Sexual Behavior in the Human Male* (Philadelphia: Saunders, 1948); A. C. Kinsey, W. Pomeroy, C. Martin, and P. Gebhard, *Sexual Behavior in the Human Female* (Philadelphia: Saunders, 1953); and Morton Hunt, *Sexual Behavior in the 1970's* (Chicago: Playboy Press, 1974).

22. See Philip Blumstein and Pepper Schwartz, *American Couples* (New York: William Morrow, 1983).

23. DeLameter and MacCorquodale (see note 20) report that 58 percent of men and 82 percent of women held standards of abstinence or a double standard, respectively in 1959, but the relative percentages had declined to 5 percent and 14 percent by 1973.

24. These data are drawn from the National Opinion Research Center General Social Surveys. For further information on the sampling and data collection, see James A. Davis, Principal Investigator, Tom W. Smith, Director and Co-Principal Investigator, *General Social Surveys, 1972–1988: Cumulative Codebook* (Chicago: National Opinion Research Center, 1988).

25. For more on abortion attitudes throughout the 1960s, see the Judith Blake article cited in note 5.

Part III
Families and the Future

9

Can We Predict the Future
of Family Life?

Throughout this book we have been exploring the question, "Is the family in trouble?" When this issue is raised, often it is not truly a question about the current state of family life, rather it reflects a concern for the future. Each of us is concerned about our own family life or that of the next generation. What will families be like over the next decade? Will families still exist in the next century? What are the chances that I will get divorced? How many grandchildren will I have?

In this chapter I will make some predictions about the future of families in the United States. These forecasts are based on the evidence that has been reviewed throughout the book and are guided by a number of principles that I first learned under the tutelage of Gerhard Lenski at the University of North Carolina at Chapel Hill.[1]

Nine Guiding Principles for Predicting the Future of Family Life

1. *Any predictions that we make about the future must be probabilistic rather than deterministic.* Statistical relationships in the social world are seldom perfect. In chapter 6, for example, it was argued that there has been a historical correlation between marital status and work status for women in this country. This correlation has been changing over time. The relationship was never deterministic—even in the nineteenth century, there were married women who had professional careers, and there were single women who did not work outside the home. Just as empirical relationships in current data are probabilistic, any predictions about the future must be placed in probabilistic terms. Some predictions will be more certain than others.

2. *The near future is more easily predictable than the distant future.* Any projections about family change will be much more accurate for the next decade than for the next century. Similarly, it will be easier to predict the nature of family life at the turn of the next century than it will

be to talk about families in the year 2050. I would, therefore, be quite confident about my predictions for divorce, marriage, and birth rates as well as the labor force participation of women throughout the 1990s. I would be much less confident of any predictions about families at the end of the twenty-first century.

3. *It is important to carefully check on the assumptions of any predictions that are made, including the definitions that are used by the person(s) making the predictions.* In terms of family life, it is critical to know how the family is defined and how variables related to family change are measured. For example, if the family is defined as a married couple with children and one adult male wage-earner, predictions about the future of family life will be radically different than if other definitions are used.

4. *The future is, to a substantial degree, an extension of the past.* As I suggested in the first chapter of this book, to understand the present or the future of family life in the United States, we must understand the past. Most of the changes in family life have not been radical departures from the past, rather they have been extensions of trends in the data that are related to our continued movement from an agricultural society to an industrial society. As a result, predictions that I make in this chapter are based on long-term trends in family variables as well as on recent shifts in these trends.

5. *Extrapolation of trends in the data is not enough; it is important to understand what forces resist or encourage these trends.* While the fourth rule is a central guiding principle, it is critical to note that predictions should not merely extend trends from the past, but must be based on an *understanding* of these trends. We must ask questions about the causes of the trends and how the many changes examined in this book are closely interrelated with one other.

6. *It is easier to predict demographic and technological trends than it is to predict ideological and political trends.* In general, social scientists have a much better understanding of the causes and consequences of demographic and technological change. Mortality levels, for example, are closely linked to a host of variables. Among the most important predictors of mortality levels in a society are nutrition, access to medical care, sanitation, and social variables such as education and income, which are correlated with all of these. Thus, unless there are radical changes in any of these variables or changes in the cause of death, demographers can quite confidently predict levels of mortality for the rest of this century, taking into account new medical discoveries and other changes in our society. Two examples of changes in the cause of death that might substantially affect these predictions would be a nuclear war, which would radically alter the physical environment, or a major epidemic, such as that which some have suggested may result from HIV infection and AIDS.

Changes in political attitudes seem to follow less predictable patterns. In the late 1960s, few social analysts would have dreamed that both Presidential candidates in 1980 would be Born-Again Christians. The data on abortion attitudes reviewed in chapter 8 suggest that changes in the makeup of the Supreme Court as well as the political power of various special interest groups may cause significant shifts in the overall distribution of attitudes toward moral and political issues that are related to family life.

7. *It is often easier to predict future problems than it is to suggest adequate solutions to those difficulties.* We currently know, for example, that the proportion of the U.S. population over the age of seventy-five is increasing. This change has many implications for the ability of government social programs to adequately provide for elderly Americans. Further, medical data indicate that as age increases, people are much more likely to suffer from chronic and catastrophic illnesses.[2] This is precisely the type of illness for which our current system of privately funded medical insurance is least able to adequately provide. This gap between the medical needs of elderly Americans and the ability of insurance programs to provide the care will increase. That problem is almost certain. The possible effective remedies of the situation are less clear.

8. *It is often easier to predict what will not happen than what will.* The best illustration of this principle is the level of divorce. I can predict with absolute confidence that the divorce rate will *not* decrease substantially over the next decade. I can also predict that the divorce rate is not likely to substantially increase in that same time period. All the factors that have been linked with the historical increase in the rate of marital dissolution will continue through the rest of this century, and the best estimate is that our society will continue to have high levels of marital dissolution (with similarly high rates of marriage and remarriage).

9. *Finally, some of the most useful predictions about the future are self-defeating.* Many of the prophets of doom have a purpose—they hope to sensitize people to social problems that are demanding our attention.[3]

After discussing some predictions for the future of family life using these nine principles, I will conclude the chapter with some additional suggestions for how we can best move toward a complete understanding of our lives and our families in this rapidly changing world.

Some Predictions About the Future of Family Life in the United States

The order in which I make these predictions roughly follows the organization of this book. Suggestions about demographic change come first, followed by a discussion of changes in gender roles. Next, I turn to change in family issues related to sexuality. Finally, I conclude with reflections on the importance of technological change and family life in the future.

Demographic Change and Family Life

Household Size and Rural/Urban Residence. Chapter 2 reviewed the historic decline in household size linked with the movement from an agricultural to an industrial society. The increase in the proportion of households containing only one or two individuals will likely continue well into the future. Despite continued increases in the cost of maintaining separate households, for most Americans, living in one's own household is a value held in high esteem.

The average household size will continue to vary, however, by a number of social characteristics within each cohort. Poor families tend to have higher fertility rates. Because black and Hispanic families are disproportionately represented in the lower range of socioeconomic status, the average size of black and Hispanic households will remain larger than white households. High fertility rates and continued migration from Mexico and Latin America will also mean that the overall proportion of the families that are Hispanic will increase substantially by the turn of the century.

While there has been some redistribution of the population away from central cities in recent years, it is not likely that this signals any major shift in the general direction of the residential distribution of families. In the future, very small proportions of each cohort will reside on farms and in rural areas. Changes in residence will much more likely involve movement from urban to suburban areas (or *vice versa*) and changes in the regional residence of families. The past three decades have involved a massive migration from the inner cities of the industrial Northeast to the sunbelt cities of the Southeast, Southwest, and West.[4] In the future, this type of internal migratory pattern will be heavily influenced by factors such as fuel prices, the availability of water and other resources, and job markets in different regions of the country.

Continued Mortality Decline and Some of Its Implications. Evidence indicates that mortality rates will continue to decline, but it is unlikely that revolutionary changes in the average expectation of life at birth will occur. Medical advances in the treatment of cancer and heart disease will likely contribute to an extended life expectancy in a small, cumulative manner, with successive cohorts enjoying better and better life chances.

As noted in the list of rules above, this general prediction must be modified if any major changes occur in the physical or social environment (such as a major nuclear accident, which results in contamination of large numbers of people, or wars that kill a significant proportion of the population, or the emergence of any new disease). While it is too early to know the extent of its impact, the spread of the HIV epidemic and its devastating repercussions on mortality rates in the early ages may modify any predictions about the average life expectation of future cohorts. Because of the sophistication of current medicine, it is likely that this impact will be limited to a relatively restricted range of cohorts—those exposed to the virus before the discovery of a vaccine to combat the virus in its various forms.[5]

We must take care not to underestimate the impact of this epidemic. AIDS has quickly become one of the leading causes of what demographers call "years of potential life lost" (YPLL). This measure indicates the number of potential productive years before the age of sixty-five that are lost to a particular disease. By 1992, AIDS will very likely be the number one cause of YPLL for men in the United States, and the number two cause overall.[6]

As noted in chapter 3, the continued increase in average life expectation has many implications for family life. Couples who marry can expect to spend many more years together in marriage than previous cohorts, and this time will continue to increase. Since women tend to outlive men, large proportions of elderly women can expect to live at least some of their later life course as widows. Throughout the century, the difference in life expectation between the sexes has increased, but recent changes in the smoking behavior of women may mean that these differences will begin to decline in the near future.[7] In the past, men were much more likely to smoke than women. The sex difference is much smaller in younger cohorts.

One of the most significant results of continued mortality declines is the growth of the proportion of the population over the age of seventy-five (the older old). The importance of this change cannot be underestimated. The political power of this group will increase over time. Indeed, there is ample evidence that the elderly have fared well in terms of government policy over the past several decades when compared with American citizens at the other end of the life course—children.[8]

The increasing number of people in the older old category of the population has implications not only for the political institution, but for our entire society. These implications are most obvious in the spheres of medicine and the family. As noted earlier, the older old are more likely to suffer from chronic illnesses, and the demands placed on the medical system by this growing group in the population are already raising serious questions about the current structuring of insurance and medical care in our country.

The financial responsibility for this care, as well as demands for emotional and social support, usually fall on the family. As chapter 4 pointed out, it is now the norm that middle-aged couples have at least one of their elderly parents alive. Family members at this stage in the life course face new responsibilities and decisions, particularly if catastrophic illness renders an elderly parent unable to care for himself or herself. One negative result I predict for the future is an increase in both the awareness and the incidence of elder abuse. Already in the 1980s there has been a heightened consciousness of maltreatment of elderly Americans (both inside the home and outside the family in institutions). The importance of this social problem will increase in the future, as more and more families have elderly members who survive well into their eighties and nineties.

Marriage, Divorce, and Remarriage. Marriage and divorce rates will continue to remain high. There is no evidence of change in the normative structure that views marriage as the desired state. Similarly, there is no evidence that the multiple factors that have led to a high divorce rate in this country will significantly change in the near future. In both the short-term and the long-term, I do not predict radical upward or downward shifts in the prevalence of either marriage or divorce. Remarriage will continue to be popular and will likely follow more institutionalized patterns in the future, as our culture develops standard ways of defining and coping with blended families.[9] If there is any directional trend in divorce rates, it will likely be upward. As noted below, the future will likely have more and more dual earner couples. These couples spend less time together than those who work less combined hours. Marital satisfaction is higher when couples spend more time together, so as the number of dual-earner couples increases, satisfaction may decline.[10]

Cohabitation. Evidence over the past several decades seems to indicate that cohabitation of couples before marriage will continue its popularity and may spread to larger proportions of the population as a prelude to matrimony. It does *not* seem likely, however, that cohabitation will replace marriage as the traditional form of adult relationship, nor will it emerge as an alternative pattern for substantial proportions of American couples.[11]

Changes in Gender Roles Inside and Outside the Family

Increase in Marital Role Options. Diversity is the key to understanding the past, present, and future of marital roles in this country. While the image may be that women in the past stayed home and raised children, data presented in earlier chapters make it abundantly clear that the true picture is much more complex than this. The Women's Movement of the 1960s and 1970s has certainly had a major impact on social attitudes about the proper roles of men and women both inside and outside the home. Nonetheless, no single model of family life or gender roles has emerged that accurately describes the diversity of options available to young cohorts of men and women entering marriage today.

All trends in the data suggest that women of all marital statuses will continue to enter the labor force in larger and larger numbers throughout their adult lives. Dual-earner families are already the norm, and this pattern will continue well into the next century. Change in attitudes and behavior will be both gradual and cumulative, as it has been in the past.

Over the next several decades, we can expect to see more and more women entering the professions, as well as many who will be employed in clerical and other service occupations that have traditionally been defined as female employment. Accompanying this change will be a significant increase in the number of *dual-career* families, in which both spouses view their employment as a career, rather than the more common dual-earner families of today.

This increase in professional women may mean a gradual increase in the proportion of the population remaining single as well as continued declines in fertility. Certainly it will mean a continuation of the delay in age at first marriage and delays in the birth of the first child, which have been seen over the past several decades. Both men and women will spend more of their adult lives in the context of a family life that will have fewer years with children, fewer young adult years in marriage, and more years when both spouses are working. Significant numbers of people are likely to spend many of their adult years in an unmarried state—either as never-married or formerly married. It is important to stress that this is *not* a new pattern, as noted in chapter 6. Rather, those who are remaining never-married are doing so for a different set of cultural reasons, and those who are formerly married are much more likely to be in that state because of divorce rather than the death of a spouse.

Increasing Variation in Individual Life Styles. The increase in dual-career and dual-earner couples should not be interpreted as signaling the extinction of what has been considered a more traditional family, where the wife is not employed or her job remains secondary to that of her husband. To the contrary, both of these patterns will continue to exist.

Just as in the past, many families in the future will choose a pattern in which one spouse devotes most of his or her attention to the raising of children. In the past this has almost exclusively been the wife, and it will likely continue to be the woman for many years in the future. Even in

Sweden, where legal equality is guaranteed to the extent of allowing paternity as well as maternity leave, most couples choose to have the wife take leave from employment rather than the husband.[12] In the future, however, it will become more socially acceptable (if not much more common) for the husband to limit his working hours and devote the extra time to child-rearing, while his spouse works in her career full-time. My prediction, however, is that this change will be extremely gradual—much more gradual than the changes that have occurred over the past two decades in attitudes toward women's roles outside the family. We have very strong cultural norms suggesting that it is the responsibility of the male to provide for his family. In the 1950s, when a woman worked it was sometimes seen as a reflection of her husband's failure to live up to this duty. The past several decades have seen major shifts in this type of attitude concerning women's work outside the home, but men who would choose to stay home and raise children while their wives support them are still viewed with great suspicion.

Just as marital roles within past cohorts have varied by such factors as ethnicity, race, and social class, future differences in how couples organize their married lives will likely be patterned differentially by race, class, and ethnicity. A working class family, for example, will be much more likely to have a role structure that is dual-earner, while spouses in a professional couple will be much more likely to define their situation as a dual-career family.

Increasing diversity will also be a hallmark of the lives of individuals who are not in their first marriage. Data from the past several decades indicate that there has been an increase in the number of women (both never-married and formerly married) who are having children outside of marriage. The rapid increase in the number of very young unmarried mothers in recent years is indeed a major social problem. The quality of life and economic outlook for both the mother and the child in such situations is often bleak.

The increase in divorce and remarriage noted above also means that many people in the future will be spending some of their adult lives (both with and without children) in a state of non-marriage. Most of these people will remarry, resulting in various forms of blended families. Others may enter into relationships other than marriage. Some of those who are formerly married as well as some who are never-married will be in relationships with people of the same sex. While the last chapter indicated that there has been little change in attitudes about the moral acceptability of homosexuality, there *does* appear to be change in the proportion of the U.S. population that supports legal protection of the rights of homosexuals. Legal changes extending the rights of homosexuals (including legalization of homosexual relationships) will not occur quickly, and indeed this will be one topic that will remain controversial throughout the rest of this century and well into the next. As noted in the last chapter, HIV infection and AIDs may have an important impact here as well, although it is difficult to predict the nature of its role. The spread of HIV infection has certainly increased the open discussion of homosexuality. Deaths of prominent Americans from a variety of occupations have helped to explode some of the myths about the nature and distribution of homosexuality in our society. These two factors would lead one to predict that the social acceptance of homosexuality may increase over the next several decades. On the other side, however, to the extent that AIDS is defined as a disease of deviants that has spread to innocent victims, the HIV epidemic may cause an increase in negative attitudes about homosexual behavior.[13]

Technological Change and Family Life

The Importance Of Technology. As indicated at the beginning of this book, the theoretical perspective that has guided this analysis emphasizes the role of technology in social change. Most of the trends that have been discussed in this book can be linked either directly or indirectly to the general transformation of our society from an agricultural to an industrial economic base. While technological change can be viewed at this broadest level, it is also instructive to examine more specific changes in technology and their impact on family life.

Changes in contraceptive technology, for example, have likely contributed to the transformation of men's and women's work and family roles since the early 1950s. Parenthood can now be viewed as a choice—a concept that was quite foreign for cohorts of women and men a century ago.

Many of the most obvious examples of technological innovations that have transformed family life are found in the area of medicine. Much of the change in mortality discussed at several points in the book can be directly linked to changes in medical technology. In the future, medical technology will continue to be an area that has profound implications for families.

An Increase in Moral Choices. Illustrations of this importance of medical advances can be found at both ends of the life course. In recent decades, a combination of developments in the medical field means that new moral choices exist for expectant parents. Science is moving closer to giving parents the ability to choose the sex of their child.[14] Genetic engineering may actually allow parents to choose other characteristics of their offspring. This possibility raises many new moral issues never before faced by families.

Some of the possibilities of this type of moral complexity have already been indicated in the popular press. Amniocentesis can be used to determine if a fetus has Down's Syndrome. A couple in Boston discovered that one of their twins had Down's and one did not. Intrauterine surgery has been perfected to the extent that they could elect to abort the child with Down's while allowing the other child to grow to full-term and have a normal birth.

At the other end of the life course, technology has also raised new moral issues for the family. With the help of respirators and other more complex machines, it is now possible to keep a human being alive long after their brain has died and long after a person would have died without the aid of modern medical science. Like the example given above, the set of ethical issues raised by the artificial extension of life did not face families in the past.

The social and natural sciences cannot decide these complex moral issues. They are decisions that will be made by individuals and families based on their personal religious and ethical convictions, subject to the laws of the land. Indeed, another area of change will be in laws affecting those family decisions.

Legal Changes in a Complex World. A final prediction I have for the future is that the number of legal issues related to family life will increase. Many of these will be related to the technological changes in medicine mentioned previously. Should abortion be legal when the child has a high probability of having some type of birth defect? (As noted in the last chapter, most Americans think that the answer to this first question is yes.) Should euthanasia be legal? Who has the legal right to decide to terminate the life of an elderly family member? Can a person make that decision for himself or herself? Will such a determination be honored when he or she is no longer capable of making an informed decision?

Other legal issues related to the family have already been in the courts—often with no clear precedent being set. Among these issues are questions relating to the marital rape exemption (in many states, it is legally impossible for a man to rape his wife, since it is her legal responsibility to be sexually available to her spouse), the legal and financial responsibility between cohabiting couples who split up, and the legal status of homosexual unions.[15]

Two less obvious examples resulting, again, from changes in medical technology have to do with sexuality. A recent case argued the inheritance rights of fertilized eggs that had been frozen. A second recent case involves someone in the middle of the life course. In late 1984, the U.S.

Postal Service was sued by a woman whose job offer had been withdrawn when she indicated that she planned on having a sex change. (In actuality, the applicant was a man when he applied for the job, but is now legally a woman.)[16]

As in the case of these ethical issues, social science cannot make a judgment about the merits of cases such as these. My point here is that radically different types of legal issues will be raised in the future because of technological changes that affect family life.

Will The Family Survive?

Thus, after all of these predictions, we return to the question with which we started the book. Will the family survive? My simple answer to that question is, "Yes, there is no doubt." But that answer does not do justice to the complexity of family change. Instead, we must take stock of some of the lessons learned from this exploration of family life in the past, present, and future.

- *First, we must think in terms of families, rather than a monolithic conception of "the family."* Diversity has always characterized family life in the United States, and that diversity will continue and thrive well into the next century.

- *Second, much of the diversity in how an individual experiences family life is linked to issues of race, class, and gender.* To focus on middle-class families, the experience of one sex, or the family life of one racial or ethnic group will lead to a serious misunderstanding of the nature of families in our country.

- *Third, most of the changes we can expect in family life over the next several decades are a continuation of long-term trends.* There will be few major changes in families in the United States that are not an extension of transformations that have been occurring over the past century as we have moved beyond the Industrial Revolution and entered the post-industrial age.

- *Fourth, none of the modifications in family life can be understood in isolation.* Each change must be placed within social and historical context. This book has illustrated the complexity of the interrelationships between a number of variables that have combined to create a revolution in family life over the past century.

- *Fifth, the family is not dying, it is changing.* Marriage and family life remain popular and will continue to thrive in the future. The structure and content of family life may be different for each cohort as individuals and families adapt to a world of rapid social change.

Conclusions—the Place of American Families in the World Community

I would like to conclude this final chapter with two observations that should guide any analysis of the health of the American family. While they differ in content, they are my addition to the list of Gerhard Lenski's principles for predicting the future presented at the opening of this chapter.

1. *Whether we are interpreting the past, evaluating the present, or predicting the future, it is important to place our situation in world context.* I have chosen in this book to concentrate on ways in which the data suggest that family life in this country is healthy. There are several reasons for this choice. First, a focus on problems in the contemporary family (such as family violence, drug abuse, teen pregnancy, and the high divorce rate) can blind us to the broader historical picture that suggests that much of family life today is stronger than in the past. Second, while it is undeniably the case that social problems such as drug abuse and family violence are critical issues deserving our attention and resources, long-term historical data are not of the quality that allows a careful analysis of trends in some of these variables. (How can we measure and compare, for example, the relative impact of loss of a parent to death in 1890 to the loss of a parent to divorce in 1990?)

Perhaps of most importance to my point here, however, is a third reason. When placed in world context, we must remember that we are the privileged. While poverty is a problem plaguing many American families, in the broader context we are clearly one of the richest nations in all the world. The types of homes we live in, the food, clothing, medical care, and transportation at our disposal are all beyond the dreams of most families worldwide. Our expectation of life is among the world's highest, and our expectations of what we will receive out of life are also among the world's highest. Children born into families in this country are indeed born into a world of privilege.

I am not saying this to suggest that we should not put resources into the problems of the poor in this country, or that we should ignore social issues such as teenage pregnancy or the impact of divorce on families. Quite to the contrary. Because we are the richest nation in the world, it is appalling that over the past two decades the gap between the rich and the poor families in this country has increased rather than decreased, and that roughly twenty countries have infant mortality rates lower than the United States.[17] It is precisely *because* children in this country are born into the richest families of the world that we should set our standards high and work toward solutions of the problems facing families in modern America.

We must also place our predictions in world context, because we live in a world community that is interdependent. While the outlook for the future of families in the United States may be positive, it cannot be divorced from the massive problems of poverty, overpopulation, and civil unrest that face much of the globe. Although this book has focused on families in this country, any complete analysis must move beyond those political boundaries created by human beings and move to the world community. The family of fourteen crushed into a small overcrowded flat in Hong Kong, the child starving in the desert of central Africa, and the woman begging on the street in Bombay to feed her children are all part of the human family. Their problems are our problems. Ultimately, the resources of the planet are limited and the long-term future of family life in this country is linked to the solution of worldwide problems of massive proportions.

2. *We live within social structures and historical times that shape our lives, yet we have the power to make choices that can affect those social structures and change the future.* After reading a book like this, you may be left with a sense of helplessness. All of the many changes in family life seem to be interconnected, and the inexorable forces of history and technological change seem to have determined how individual lives and families will be structured.

Individuals make choices throughout their lives, however, and families and other groups make decisions that structure the present and the future, while building on the legacy from the past. One of the principles at the beginning of this chapter suggested that future trends in attitudes and ideology are more difficult to predict than patterns in some other variables. While a social scientist who wants to accurately predict the future may be bothered by this introduction of uncertainty, in actuality it is a reflection of the importance of individual choice.

In this chapter I have suggested a number of new legal and moral choices that will face families over the next several decades. Each of us will find many times in our lives when we have the power to shape the direction of the future of families in the United States. We will likely be asked to vote on issues related to family life. In our jobs we may face decisions that will affect not only our own families, but others as well. (One example that comes to mind is employer-sponsored childcare for employees.) We will have many opportunities to volunteer our time, efforts, and resources to agencies and charities that are attempting to deal with many of the problems facing families today. It is my hope that the information in this book may provide a broader perspective from which to make these decisions.

I would like to conclude by linking these two final propositions. While I have taken a position throughout this book that there are a large number of historical trends in the data indicating the health of family life, it is also true that one general trend has caused great concern among some analysts of the family.

The combined effect of a number of the trends that have been traced in this book has been a considerable increase in the amount of freedom and privacy available to individuals within the family context. Household size is smaller, marriage is less binding on the individual, and a broader range of behaviors is seen as permissible both inside and outside the marriage bond. Earlier in the book I suggested that one result of this rise in family privacy may be a lessening of traditional gender roles.

In and of itself, more privacy and freedom may be viewed as positive, but there are costs as well as benefits. It is possible, for example, that this increased privacy has allowed negative behaviors, such as child, spouse, and elder abuse to take on more intensity and remain undetected by the surrounding community for longer periods of time. It is difficult to find direct measures to support this type of contention, but I would also suggest that an increase in individual choice has often led to an increase in concern for the self over others. Freedom without responsibility is anarchy, and critics of the modern family fear that the individual has come to be more important than relationships and family life, that self-interest has replaced commitment.

This is a powerful argument, and I would suggest that while it may overstate the case, it must not be ignored. If we take the final two propositions in this chapter seriously, then it becomes clear that commitment must be developed and nurtured in modern society if humanity is to survive. That commitment must be not only to one's own personal relationships and family life, but to the broader human family. We live in an interdependent world community, and as individuals, families, and a nation, we must use our power to shape social structures in a way that will build a strong future for all of the human family.

Notes

1. A fuller discussion of several of these principles can be found in Gerhard Lenski and Jean Lenski, *Human Societies: An Introduction to Macrosociology*, 5th ed. (New York: McGraw-Hill, 1987). The more complete list used here is drawn from notes taken in Dr. Gerhard Lenski's graduate seminar on neoevolutionary theory at the University of North Carolina at Chapel Hill in 1977. I want to thank him for permission to use them in this book.

2. See Robert Atchley, *Social Forces and Aging*, 4th ed. (Belmont, CA: Wadsworth Publishing Company, 1984), p. 76.

3. In his course lectures, Dr. Gerhard Lenski referred to this final principle as the "Jeremiah principle," and used the example of George Orwell's *1984*, which

was designed to alert people to the dangers of government interference in personal life.

4. Recent data on trends in suburban movement of the population can be found in Barry Edmonston and Thomas M. Guterbock, "Is Suburbanization Slowing Down? Recent Trends in Population Deconcentration in U.S. Metropolitan Areas," *Social Forces* 62(4):905–925, 1984. For more on the expansion of Sun Belt cities, see Peter R. Gluck and Richard J. Meister, *Cities in Transition* (New View: New York Viewpoints, 1979).

5. An excellent review of the history of medical understanding of the AIDS virus and the epidemic is June E. Osborn's "The AIDS Epidemic: An Overview of the Science," *Issues in Science and Technology* (Winter 1986):39–55.

6. For more on this measure and the role of AIDS in mortality shifts, see James Curran, Harold W. Jaffe, Ann M. Hardy, W. Meade Morgan, Richard M. Selik, and Timothy J.Dondero, "Epidemiology of HIV infection and in AIDS in the United States," *Science* 239 (1988):610–639. This information is also based on a lecture given by James Curran, entitled "AIDS Update," at the preconference workshop on AIDS at the annual meetings of the National Council on Family Relations, Philadelphia, Fall 1988.

7. For further information on sex differences in mortality and their patterning over time, see Edward L.Kain, "Trends in the Demography of Death," in Hannelore Wass, Felix M. Berardo, and Robert A. Neimeyer (eds.), *Dying: Facing the Facts*, 2nd ed. (New York: Hemisphere, 1988), pp. 79–96.

8. In his article, "Children and the Elderly in the U.S.," *Scientific American* 251(6):44–49, December 1984, Samuel H. Preston convincingly illustrates how government spending and measures of well-being indicate that the elderly have improved their situation since 1960, while chidren's positions have deteriorated.

9. See Andrew Cherlin, "Remarriage as an Incomplete Institution," *American Journal of Sociology* 84(3),1978.

10. These relationships are documented in Paul William Kingston and Steven L. Nock, "Time Together Amoung Dual-Earner Couples," *American Sociological Review* 52(June 1987):391–400.

11. Cohabitation has a long tradition in Sweden, Denmark, Norway, Germany, and Ireland. Rates have varied over time, however, with cohabitation becoming more popular in Sweden, for example, in the early 1970s. For more on these patterns, see Jan Trost, "Married and Unmarried Cohabitation: A Case of Sweden, with Some Comparisons," *Journal of Marriage and the Family* 37(1975):677–682; and "A Renewed Social Institution: Non-marital Cohabitation," *Acta Sociologica* 21 (1978):303–315.

12. See Jan Trost, "Parental Benefits—A Study of Men's Behavior and Views," *Current Sweden* (Stockholm: The Swedish Institute (June):1–7.

13. A number of authors have discussed the implications of the social definition of AIDS as a disease of deviant groups. See Edward Albert, "Illness and Deviance: The Response of the Press to AIDS," in Douglas A. Feldman and Thomas M. Johnson (eds.), *The Social Dimensions of AIDS: Methods and Theory* (New York: Praeger, 1986), pp. 163–178; and "Acquired Immune Deficiency Syndrome: The Victim and the Press," *Studies in Communications* 3 (1986):135–158. A book length discussion of the social definition of AIDS and the resultant

responses to the disease in Dennis Altman's *AIDS in the Mind of America: The Social, Political, and Psychological Impact of a New Epidemic* (Garden City, NY: Anchor Press/Doubleday, 1986).

14. Bernice Lott reviews the literature on sex preferences for children in the United States in chapter 2 of *Women's Lives: Themes and Variations in Gender Learning* (Monterey, CA: Brooks/Cole Publishing Company, 1987). Research indicates a strong preference for boys. If it becomes possible for parents to choose the sex of their child, this may cause an unusual sex distribution in the population.

15. For more on laws concerning marital rape, see David Finkelhor and Kersti Yllo, *License to Rape: The Sexual Abuse of Wives* (New York: Holt, Rinehardt, 1985).

16. For more on this second case, see "Applicant Who Changed Sex Sues Postal Service Over Job Offer," *The Washington Post*, Sunday, December 2, 1984, p. B9.

17. See Urie Bronfenbrenner, "The Changing Family in a Changing World: America First?" Paper presented at an internation symposium sponsored by UNESCO on *Children and Families in a Changing World*, Munich, November (1982): 22–25. For more information on infant mortality see John R. Week's *Population* (Belmont, CA: Wadsworth, 1989).

Index

Abortion: attitudes toward, 41–42, 122–123, 131–132, 141; historical rates for, 121–122; laws concerning, 10, 121; legal and moral issues of, 148

Adultery: and cross-cultural patterns, 127, 128. *See also* Extramarital sexual behavior

Aging: and insurance problems, 141, 143–144; and marriage, 72–73; race and sex differentials for, 62–63. *See also* Mortality rates

Agricultural decline: and changes in family life, 33–36, 37–38

AIDS: and attitudes toward homosexuality, 124, 147; and mortality rate predictability, 140; and residence differential, 64

Aron, Cindy, 88

Auchmuty, Rosemary, 82

Baby boom: and cohort analysis, 24–26

Bane, Mary Jo, 10, 79

Bem, Sandra, 110

Bernard, Jessie, 84 85

Bernard, Richard M., 83

Black families: fertility rates for, 49; and household size, 142; and household structure, 8, 50; and mortality rate, 64–65; and orphanhood, 58–59; and sibling loss, 57

Blake, Judith, 122

Blumstein, Philip, 129

Boas, Franz, 19, 20

Brumberg, Joan Jacobs, 84

Cambridge Group for the History of Population and Social Structure, 20

Cann, Arnie, 111

Carney, L. S., 108

Cherlin, Andrew J., 71

Chicago School of Sociology, 20

Child abuse: and privacy, 152

Childe v. Gordon, 21

Childhood mortality, 37, 55–56, 57. *See also* Infant mortality

Children: and labor force participation by married women, 98; and orphanhood, 57–58; and sibling loss, 56–57. *See also* Fertility rates

Cohabitation: as alternative pattern, 74, 144; and legal issues, 148

Cohort analysis: and family life, 22–26; and farm families (intra-cohort variation), 38–43; and social change, 36–38

Condry, John, 111

Condry, Sandra, 111

Contraceptive technology: and divorce rate, 72; and social change, 147

Cross-cultural perspective: on divorce, 71; and gender roles, 107, 108; on human sexuality, 126–129

Crude Divorce Rate (CDR), 70

Cultural lag: and social institutions, 10–11

Culture: and gender differences, 107–108, 109–115; and sex stereotyping, 110–113

Demographic changes: and farm
versus non-farm families, 41–43;
in fertility, 47–51; in mortality,
47–48, 51–65; predictions for,
140, 141–144
Dichotomization: of sexuality,
128–129. *See also* Socialization;
Domesticity, cult of
Divorce: attitudes toward, 71–72
Divorce rate: and family survival,
69–73; historical patterning of,
5–6; predictions for, 141, 144,
146; and urbanization, 35
Domestic service: and household
composition, 50; as occupation for
women, 94, 95
Domesticity, cult of, 82–86
Doyle, Donald C., 112
Dual-career families: future of, 145,
146
Dual-earner families: future of, 144,
145, 146; rates of, 79
Dublin, Thomas, 82

Economic functions: and family life,
17–18; of farm families, 38–39
Economic value: and women's work,
114–115
Education, higher: and baby boomers,
25–26; and marital status of
women, 83–86
Elder, Glen H., 16, 27, 37, 99
Elder abuse, 144; and privacy, 152
Ethnicity: and occupational choices
for women, 93–95
Evolutionism: and family study,
18–20; and social change, 21. *See
also* Neoevolutionary theory
Extramarital sexual behavior:
attitudes toward, 41, 124–125,
131; and cross-cultural perspective,
127; rates of, 129

Family: definition and functions of,
16–18; and divorce rate, 69–73;
and historical perspective, 3–11
Family labor system: in mills, 82
Family life: and agricultural decline,
33–36, 42; and household size, 6,
48–51, 73; and mortality decline,
51–65; predictions for, 141–149;

and privacy, 50–51; in rural
settings, 38–43; and technological
change, 147–149; theoretical
approaches to, 15–30; and work
status of women, 81–86
Family Protection Act, 10
Family reconstitution, 20
Farm families: attitudinal variables in
NORC survey, 41–43;
demographic variables in NORC
survey, 40–41; and income,
38–39
Farm life: and agricultural decline,
33–36; impact of, on families, 35,
38–43
Fertility rates: for black families, 49,
56, 57; in Colonial era, 51, 72;
demographic changes in, 47–51;
and economic status, 142; and
urbanization, 35
Frankfort, Roberta, 83, 85, 86
Functionalism, structural: and family
life, 16–18; origins of, 18–20

Gender categories, 105–106
Gender differences: and culture,
106–108; development of,
109–113; and mortality rates,
62–63, 143; and self-evaluation,
112–113; and singlehood, 76
Gender roles: and dichotomization,
105–106, 109; and Family
Protection Act, 10; future changes
in, 144–147; and industrialization,
128; and occupations for women,
81–86, 87; and socialization,
113–115
Generation: concept of, 22–23
Gettys, Linda D., 111
Glenn, Norval D., 124, 125
Goode, William J., 18, 33, 70
Gutman, Herbert G., 8

Henry, Louis, 20
Hispanic population: and AIDS, 64;
and household size, 142
Historical context: and study of
families, 3–8, 20, 27
HIV infection: and attitudes about
homosexuality, 124, 131, 147; and
mortality rate predictability, 140;

About the Author

Edward L. Kain received his B. A. in sociology and religion in 1976 from Alma College in Alma, Michigan. He completed his Ph.D. in sociology at the University of North Carolina at Chapel Hill in 1980. After beginning his academic career at Cornell University, he moved on to Southwestern University in Georgetown, Texas where he is now an associate professor in the Department of Sociology. Dr. Kain is active in both the American Sociological Association (ASA) and the National Council on Family Relations. He serves on the editorial board of *Teaching Sociology* and is active in the Teaching Resources Group of the ASA. His research focuses on various aspects of social change and family life, with special emphasis on mortality trends. He is currently researching a book on the social impact of the HIV epidemic.